# The Sourcebook of Contemporary Urban Design

# The Sourcebook of Contemporary Urban Design

Francesc Zamora Mola

HARPER
DESIGN

*An Imprint of HarperCollinsPublishers*

HarperCollins books may be purchased for educational, business, or sales promotional use.
For information, please write: Special Markets Department, HarperCollins*Publishers*,
10 East 53rd Street, New York, NY 10022.

First Edition published in 2012 by
Harper Design
*An Imprint of* HarperCollins*Publishers*
10 East 53rd Street
New York, NY 10022
Tel.: (212) 207-7000
Fax: (212) 207-7654
harperdesign@harpercollins.com
www.harpercollins.com

Distributed throughout the world by
HarperCollins*Publishers*
10 East 53rd Street
New York, NY 10022
Fax: (212) 207-7654

Packaged by
LOFT Publications
Via Laietana 32, 4º, Of. 92
08003 Barcelona, Spain
Tel.: +34 932 688 088
Fax: +34 932 687 073
loft@loftpublications.com
www.loftpublications.com

Editorial coordination:
Aitana Lleonart Triquell

Editor and texts:
Francesc Zamora Mola

Art director:
Mireia Casanovas Soley

Design and layout coordination:
Claudia Martínez Alonso

Cover layout:
María Eugenia Castell Carballo

Layout:
Cristina Simó Perales

Translation:
Cillero & de Motta

ISBN: 978-0-06-211358-0

Library of Congress Control Number: 2012932387

Printed in China

# Contents

Urban landscape includes spaces that are open and public. They may or may not incorporate natural elements such as green areas and aquatic zones, or provide space for leisure activities and mass public events. They are often the physical nexus of neighborhood identity. The vital importance of urban public open spaces can be appreciated when we observe the myriad of uses that people make of these places. Motivated by the desire to enjoy the environment, they take long relaxing strolls or walk the dog, practice sports, and attend events, among other activities. As we shall see, the different types of spaces can be categorized by social typologies based on age, gender, and physical and mental ability. Furthermore, the projects included in this book show that accessibility and lighting are issues tackled by designers to allow people to move safely around public open spaces.

Urban spaces are beneficial to societies at a social level since they are open to everyone, fostering community spirit. They foster the development of children through outdoor activities that involve playing, running, and interacting. More specifically, green urban spaces provide numerous educational opportunities and contribute to maintaining biodiversity of existing natural habitats. And ultimately, they improve the conditions of the urban environment by reducing pollution and utilizing sustainable practices such as water management. Urban areas can also benefit from the economic growth engendered by urban parks and gardens, as they add value to neighborhood real estate and attract new businesses and tourism.

However, open public spaces are coming increasingly under pressure in cities as a consequence of overdevelopment and urban sprawl. As cities grow denser, we see our connection with nature grow weaker.

While it is difficult to create new green open areas in the built-up urban fabric, city governments—in collaboration with landscape architects, urbanists, and experts in various fields—can implement strategies that bring sustainable urban regeneration to the fore. With the lack of available land, which makes it difficult to create new open spaces, these efforts are often centered in the recuperation of existing infrastructures to improve city dwellers' quality of life. Examples shown in this book illustrate how cities are transforming derelict structures into parks, restoring natural habitats polluted by many years of industrial occupation, and integrating ports and waterfronts into the urban fabric to reestablish the connection between the city and the water. These projects are often implemented along with public education of the environmental value of urban spaces, which in turn will improve public health and well-being.

It is obvious that cities will continue to grow, but we can change our approach to the integration of nature in cities and find ways to develop that don't distance city dwellers from nature. The focus on reestablishing a connection with nature does not imply the slowing or restricting of development. On the contrary, if well considered, it may improve neighborhoods and encourage reinvestment.

The structure of this book is based on a typology that reflects the variety of public open spaces that make up the urban fabric. Needless to say, this typology is only one approach to organize the selected projects.

They are gardens, parks, linear parks, and plazas like the "Promenade of Light" by Tonkin Liu, an exemplary urban regeneration scheme that has resurrected a tree-lined promenade in a neglected area in the city of London. Consulted users have expressed that they feel safer on the promenade and that the improved streetscape has benefited local business. Other projects include public spaces around institutional developments such as "The City Dune" by SLA, a green and open foyer for the public and the employees of the SEB Bank in Copenhagen. Public spaces around residential developments are represented in this book, also. One example is the "Central Plaza for the Katzenbach Housing" in Zurich by Robin Winogrond Landscape Architect. This project is part of a large, high-density housing complex with landscaped courtyards incorporating vegetation, sand and water, play elements, and seating. Playgrounds, zoos, botanical gardens, and cemeteries are community assets that contribute to the quality of life. This category includes projects such as "Bahndeckel" in Munich, a new open space and playground designed by Topotek 1 in collaboration with Rosemarie Trockel and Catherine Venart. The space is built over underground train tracks and connects various parks and newly built housing complexes. Developments of infrastructures are dominant representations of contemporary urbanism. An example of this is the "Craigieburn Bypass," designed by Taylor Cullity Lethlean, Tonkin Zulaikha Greer, and Robert Owen in Melbourne. This striking intervention brings Melbourne's freeway system into focus and acts like a gateway to the city—a sign of welcome or farewell. The seafront and riverbank recuperation category includes the "Sunken Stone Garden" in Seoul by Mikyoung Kim and SeoAhn Total Landscape. In an effort to revitalize a heavily polluted, and for a long time covered, canal, the design team created a gathering space to reengage people with the historic river while addressing flood risk management. Seafront and riverside developments encompasses a selection of ambitious projects such as the "West Palm Beach Waterfront Commons." Michael Singer Studio lead the reimaging process for a cohesive waterfront that includes a main park, three event spaces, three new floating docks, shaded gardens, two community buildings, a waterfront esplanade, and an estuarine regeneration area. Finally, the last section of the book is dedicated to projects that are under construction or visionary representation of potential undertakings. The "Aranzadi Park" in Pamplona is a work in progress that began construction in 2009. It consists of the restoration of the Arga River meander dynamism. In the long term, the effects of this restoration will establish a balance between the natural cycle of the river's dynamics and the need for a recreational space for the citizens.

These are examples of innovative methods to create, manage, and maintain public open spaces. The design process of these spaces does not end when a new park is created. Rather, it is an approach to long-term problem solving that tackles barriers and considers with local conditions, culture, and human needs.

The selection of projects included in the book shows that urban landscape is not just about creating parks and gardens, but also is concerned with recuperating derelict areas and transforming them into new public spaces. The desire for a healthier lifestyle and a closer connection with nature has brought architects, landscape architects, and planners in collaboration with city communities to reclaim abandoned waterfronts, former industrial parks, toxic waste filled sites, and polluted rivers.

Public open spaces offer benefits at a social, health, environmental, and economic level, and from an urban renewal standpoint, the projects examined in the book not only improve the environment by making it more pleasant, but by doing so, they promote reinvestment, increase land value, and strengthen communities.

# GARDENS,
PARKS,
LINEAR PARKS,
AND PLAZAS

# MIAMI BEACH SOUNDSCAPE / LINCOLN PARK

Miami Beach, FL, USA   2011

West 8 delivered a park that is intimate, shady, and soft and at the same time supports the artistic atmosphere brought in by the New World Symphony Building. Lincoln Park reflects the spirit and vitality of Miami Beach and accommodates a multitude of day and night uses, either under the shade of the trees or the starlit sky. The artistic quality of the park is reinforced by a projection wall on the adjacent Symphony Hall building. This provides an ideal canvas for video artists.

A dynamic grid of white concrete pathways, at times bordered by benches of the same material, quarter the soft and undulating green topography. Aluminum pergolas, inspired by the puffy cumulus inherent to the South Florida tropical climate, provide shade and support the spectacular blooms of bougainvillea vines, marking a threshold of color at the park's entry points.

"Veils" of palm and specimen trees conceal and reveal views, further reinforcing the experience of being within an oasis. West 8 has designed a projection tower and "Ballet Bar" to house the extensive multimedia equipment contained within the park. These elements create a consistent language among the park's unique architectural elements, providing a wide range of possibilities.

**LANDSCAPE ARCHITECT**
West 8 urban design & landscape architecture

**LOCATION**
Miami Beach, FL, USA

**CLIENT**
City of Miami Beach

**COLLABORATORS**
Coastal Systems International (civil engineer), Hines (development manager), Pro Sound and Video (projection design), Douglas Wood Associates (structural engineer), Cosentini Associates (MEP engineer), Rosenberg Gardner Design (local landscape architect), Leo A. Daly (local architects)

**COMPLETION DATE**
2011

**AREA**
2.47 acres (1 ha)

**COST**
n/a

**PHOTOGRAPHER**
Robin Hill

Location map

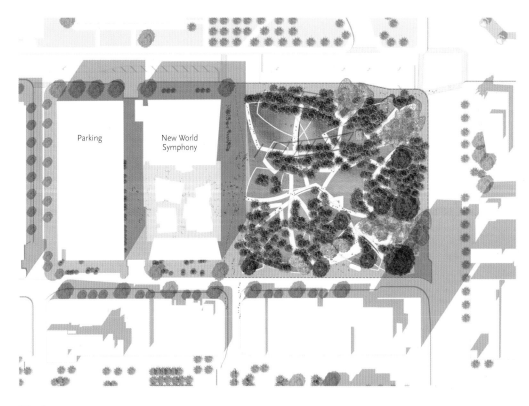

Site plan

Lincoln Park is the expression of recreation and culture. The multiple uses of the Symphony Hall Building and the outstanding architecture make the New World Symphony campus a world-class destination that marries music, design, and experience.

The sculptural pergolas echo the pattern formed by the meandering pathways. This pattern, which contrasts with the green mantle that covers the site, creates the illusion of the park being larger than it actually is.

# ORANGE COUNTY GREAT PARK

Irvine, CA, USA    (ongoing)

The Orange County Great Park is a site formerly known as the United States Marine Corps Air Station when it was still under federal ownership. In 2005, it was handed over to a developer to build the park.

The ongoing project will actually be three park experiences in one: The Great Canyon is a beautiful oasis, a place for families to picnic and for children to explore; the Wildlife Corridor is an ecological backbone with a wide variety of plant species, and wildlife; finally, the Fields and Memorial Park commemorate the history of the site as both a productive agricultural landscape and, more recently, a military base.

The development plan takes into consideration the broader strategic goals of improving regional connections, promoting sustainable practices, reflecting site history, and celebrating diverse populations and cultures within Orange County. Within an ecological context, principles of sustainability guide all aspects of the park's design. This includes habitat restoration, renewable energy generation, water quality management, and promotion of non-polluting transportation methods. Such strategies are aimed to inspire people to make changes in their own lives, thus creating a profound impact far beyond the park's boundaries.

**DESIGNERS**
Mia Lehrer + Associates & Ken Smith Workshop West

**CLIENT**
Orange County Great Park Corporation

**COLLABORATORS**
WRNS Studio, DMc Engineering, LSA Associates, Chora Creative, MR+E Metropolitan Research and Economics

**AREA**
1,347 acres

**COST**
USD 1.2 billion

**PHOTOGRAPHER**
Mia Lehrer + Associates

The comprehensive master plan for the Orange
County Great Park outlines a vision for a new kind of
park where fresh ideas for social and environmental
sustainability will be investigated and tested.

Master plan

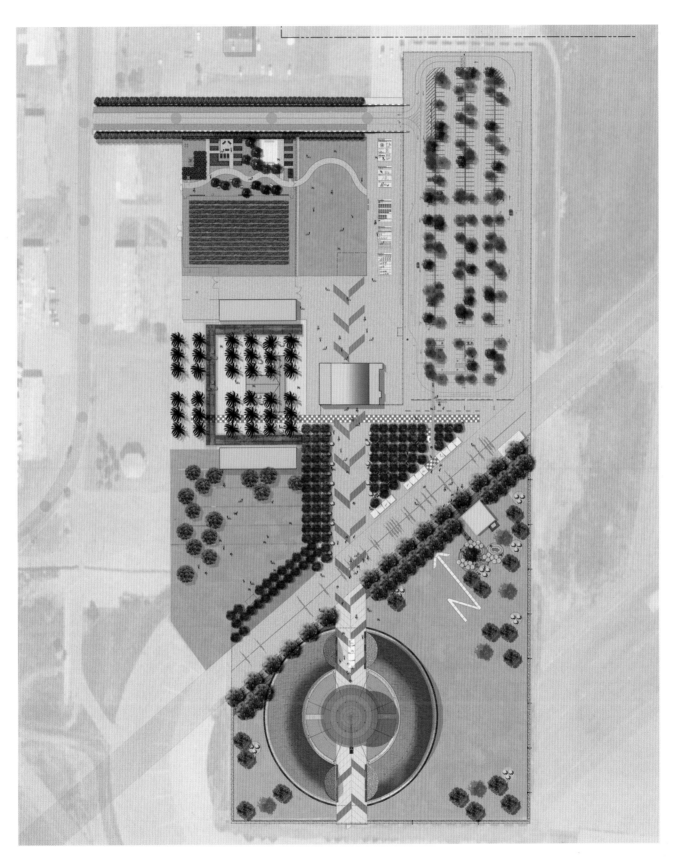

Cultural Terrace plan

The community has played an important role in creating the Great Park through meetings with stakeholder groups and a public participation campaign. The public also watches the "growing of the park" from up high in the Great Park balloon.

# RAILROAD PARK

## Birmingham, AL, USA   2010

The park is a former warehouse and brick-making site four blocks long by one block wide and was, historically, the lowest point in town. This project includes the active participation of eleven trains that slowly lumber through this downtown on tracks through a viaduct. The scheme includes a large reservoir for irrigation, which discharges through a stream and series of ponds. An 80 foot long "Rain Curtain" drops lake water off the Rail Trail Bridge into the reservoir, providing additional oxygenation. In the process, this system creates a large-scale summertime series of fountain experiences for kids as well as adults.

Needed floodwater storage is created by excavating for this water system. The excavated material is used to create a series of knolls along the "Rail Trail." The path, located atop this little mountain range, is a series of on-grade and bridge connections that allow for close-up train watching, as well as views over downtown and of the frequent large music events and parties within the park.

The park is intended to provide a civic "living room" between the downtown north of the rail viaduct, dominated by office and commercial spaces, and the downtown south of the viaduct, filled with low-rent warehouses converted into residential lofts.

**LANDSCAPE ARCHITECT**
Tom Leader Studio

**CLIENT**
City of Birmingham / Railroad Park Foundation

**COLLABORATORS**
Macknally Ross Land Design (landscape design), KVA, GA Architecture, HKW Associates, Khafra Engineering Consultants, Walter Schoel Engineering Company

**AREA**
827,640 sq ft (19 acres)

**COST**
USD 17.5 million

**PHOTOGRAPHER**
Tom Leader Studio, Jeff Newman, Sylvia Martin

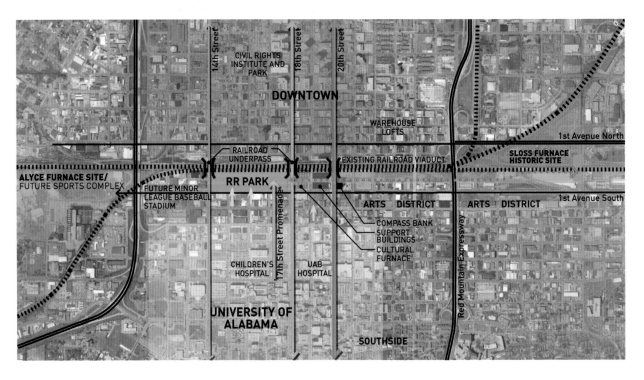

Scheme of the downtown central park and master plan of the rail corridor

An irrigation reservoir is fed by harvested water on-site as well as good-quality recycled industrial water from off-site. This water then runs through a system of streams and ponds before it is pumped back to a wetland, which in turn feeds the reservoir.

Situated in Birmingham, home of many festivals and music parties, the project is designed to provide venues for events to occur, often simultaneously. Also, movies are shown at the grass amphitheater, where people spread out on blankets and chairs for the evening.

# GOLD MEDAL PARK

## Minneapolis, MN, USA    2006

Gold Medal Park, located in the heart of Minneapolis Mills District, hearkens back to the intentions of the city founders and planners—who had the foresight to set aside open space for the area's popular Chain of Lakes and Grand Rounds Scenic Byway. As a result, they created some of the most revered and enjoyable places in the city and the metropolitan region.

The design offers an open space close to the Mississippi River and Jean Nouvel's Guthrie Theater.

Historically occupied by mills, grain elevators, and a busy rail yard on the edge of Minneapolis West Bank Mills District, the land had recently been used as a parking lot. Contamination from these past uses dictated the design, which resulted in the focal point of the park: a sculptural observation mound—32 feet high and 350 feet in diameter—with a grove of Amur maple trees and seating at the top. The mound is not only a compositional element of the park's design but also during its construction, it permitted the builders to isolate and safely contain the contamination that remained from the site's previous uses. This strategy reduced the cost of moving soil in and out of the site while and created an eye-catching centerpiece. The presence of this landform is emphasized by the Corten steel-lined paths.

**LANDSCAPE ARCHITECT**
Oslund and Associates

**LOCATION**
Minneapolis, MN, USA

**CLIENT**
Park Development Foundation

**CONSTRUCTION**
2006

**AREA**
7.5 acres

**COST**
USD 5 million

**PHOTOGRAPHER**
Michael Mingo & Oslund and Associates

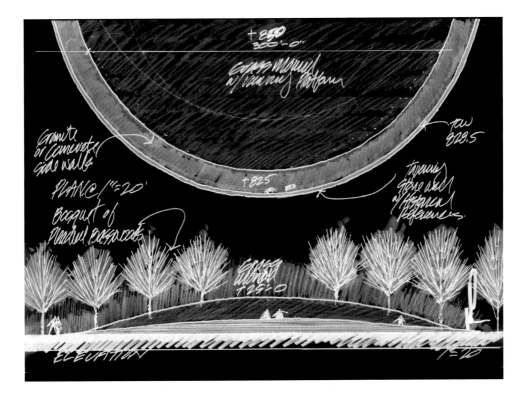

Development sketch

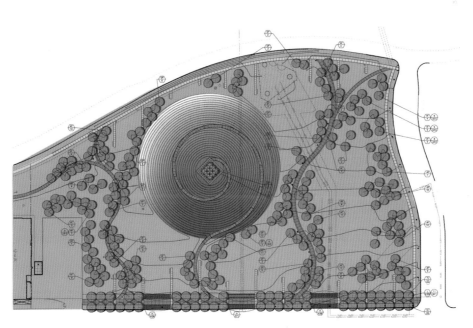

Site plan

The park includes close to 300 mature trees. The
species include maples, lindens, hackberries,
oaks, and catalpas. Twenty custom-designed
benches line the edges of the park, creating
places for visitors to relax and enjoy the views.

Blue LED lights transform the benches into lanterns at nighttime. Accompanied by other custom light features, the lighting design adds a unique ephemeral quality to the park throughout the night.

# DUBLIN GROUNDS OF REMEMBRANCE

## Dublin, OH, USA   2009

The project aimed to recognize veterans and their families. Rather than a memorial, the site is "a place for reflection, contemplation, remembrance, honor, introspection, and community gathering." The design approach defines, demarcates, and names the various components of the site. The Grounds of Remembrance, which contains the Indian Run Cemetery, is organized into three areas: Walk, Loggia, and Sycamore Grove. Together they define the limits of the grounds and choreograph the experience through the site on both ceremonial days and everyday visits. Architectural and landscape elements make reference to the cultural and natural history of the site—the cemetery, ravine forest, and limestone cliffs. Each element reinforces the physical and mental remembrance that generates personal meaning for the site while they also provide physical and metaphorical support, shelter, and guidance. The Walk focuses on the individual's journey of remembrance; the Grove provides for both wandering and large function gatherings; and the Loggia is a place of rest. Thresholds of entry are clearly marked: at Dublin Road by a bridge with the name carved into the stone pavement; at the library grounds by a gate; and at the nature walk by the break in the Guide Rail.

**ARCHITECT**
PLANT Architect

**CLIENT**
Fred Hahn, Director of Parks and Open Space
City of Dublin Parks Department

**COLLABORATORS**
Local Architect / Engineer: Jack D Walters and Associates Inc., Dublin, OH
Structural Engineer: Blackwell Bowick Engineering, Toronto, Canada
Electrical Engineer: McMullen Engineering Co., Westerville, OH
Soils Engineer: BBC&M Engineering Inc., Dublin, OH
Civil Engineer: Hull and Associates, Dublin, OH
General Contractor: McDaniels Construction, Columbus, OH
Bronze Contractor: QAF – Quality Architectural & Fabrication, Inc., Franklin, OH

**AREA**
n/a

**COST**
USD 750,000

**AWARDS**
2010 National Honor Award by the Canadian Society of Landscape Architects (CSLA)

**PHOTOGRAPHER**
PLANT Architect

45

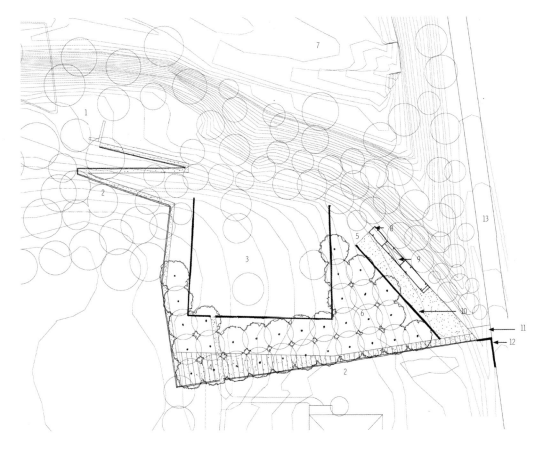

1. Limestone bench
   and Memory Wall
2. The Guide Rail
3. Indian Run Cemetery
4. The Walk
5. Flag
6. The Grove
7. Indian Run
8. Emerson Hymn
9. The Loggia
10. Limestone
    dedication wall
11. Bridge
12. Limestone entry wall
13. Dublin Road

Site plan

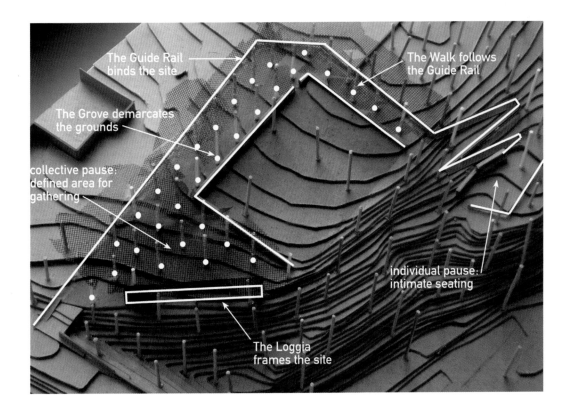

The Guide Rail binds the site

The Walk follows the Guide Rail

The Grove demarcates the grounds

collective pause: defined area for gathering

individual pause: intimate seating

The Loggia frames the site

This seemingly lightweight structure blends seamlessly with the existing parkland. This academy is one of the world's greenest museums, having scored a total of 54 points in its LEED certification audit.

46

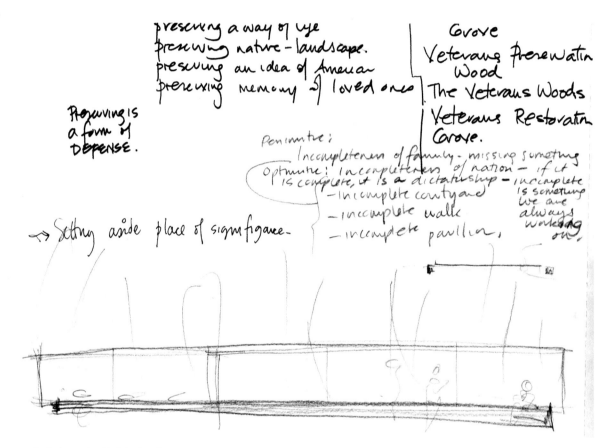

preserving a way of life
preserving nature - landscape.
preserving an idea of American
preserving memory of loved ones

Preserving is a form of DEFENSE.

Grove
Veterans Preservation Wood
The Veterans Woods
Veterans Restoration Grove.

Perimeter:
Incompleteness of family - missing something
Optimistic: Incompleteness of nation - if it is complete, it is a dictatorship - incomplete is something we are always working on.
- Incomplete courtyard
- incomplete walk
- incomplete pavilion.

→ Setting aside place of significance.

Preliminary sketch of the Loggia

View of the gathering area from the library

# TOPPILANSAARI PARK

## Oulu, Finland   2005

The park was laid out around the Finnish Housing Expo 2005 not far from wetlands, forming a central core for the relatively spread-out houses. Taking into account this environmentally sensitive location, the park accommodates paths and bicycle lanes as well as other recreational areas. It also contains a storm water system that collects rainwater and snowmelt, which are later released into the wetlands. The pavement at the intersections, which is laid in waves in reference to the nearby sea, accommodates the storm water system.

*Toppilansaari* means "Park of the Young Sailor" in Finnish. This name defined the program of two land art installations that close the southern and northern ends of the park. In the southern garden, a conceptual sunken boat is a memorial to all the young sailors who never returned to land. In the northern garden, a light "vortex" is an orientation landmark, visible like a lighthouse. The light vortex rotates in the wind, lighting up various sculptures designed by Herbert Dreiseitl, using recycled materials.

**LANDSCAPE ARCHITECT**
Atelier Dreiseitl

**CLIENT**
City of Oulu

**COLLABORATORS**
Suunnittelukeskus OY

**AREA**
75 acres (303.514 m²)

**COST**
n/a

**PHOTOGRAPHER**
Atelier Dreiseitl

Toppilansaari, a half island between the canalized
Oulu harbor entrance and the Baltic Sea, was
the site of the Finnish Housing Expo 2005.
The site's unique natural habitat has been
preserved and coexists with areas that celebrate
the past and present of the people of Oulu.

Aerial view photomontage

Site plan

# TANNER SPRINGS PARK

Portland, OR, USA   2005

The City of Portland commissioned Atelier Dreiseitl to design a park to bring some green to the rapidly expanding Pearl District in Portland. The area, which was previously a marshland dissected by the Tanner Creek and bordered by the Willamette River, was first occupied by rail yards and industry that drained the site before the dynamic mix of housing, offices, shops, and art galleries were progressively established.

Envisioned as a model of urban sustainable design, the park slopes from a meadow at the western end, through stone paths flanked with wetland plants, to a large pond at the eastern end. Also, the fact that the western end of the park is raised above street level provides a pleasant sense of separation between the park and its urban surroundings.

Storm water management is an important feature of the project: rather than directing the water runoff onto the gutter, storm water is collected in a main waterbed along the side of the park. Framing the park, a wavy wall made of 368 rails makes reference to the former industrial use of the site. The 180-foot-long wall has 99 pieces of fused glass inset with images of nature hand-painted by artist Herbert Dreiseitl.

**LANDSCAPE ARCHITECT**
Atelier Dreiseitl

**LOCATION**
Portland, OR, USA

**CLIENT**
City of Portland

**COLLABORATORS**
GreenWorks

**AREA**
1 acre

**COST**
n/a

**AWARDS**
2006 Oregon Merit Award from the American Society of Landscape Architects (ASLA)

**PHOTOGRAPHER**
Atelier Dreiseitl

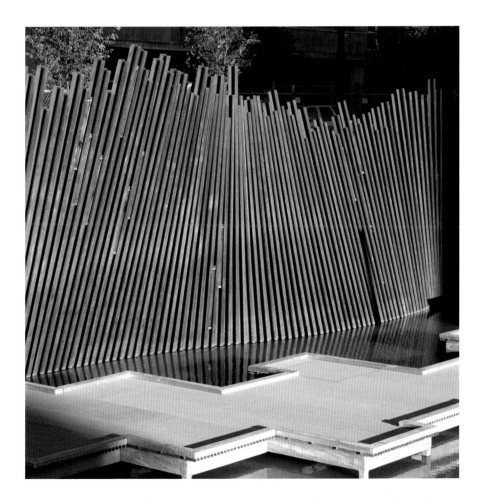

Lawn terraces along both the northern and southern edges of the park, provide seating for visitors to read, eat their lunch on a sunny day, or simply relax and observe park activity.

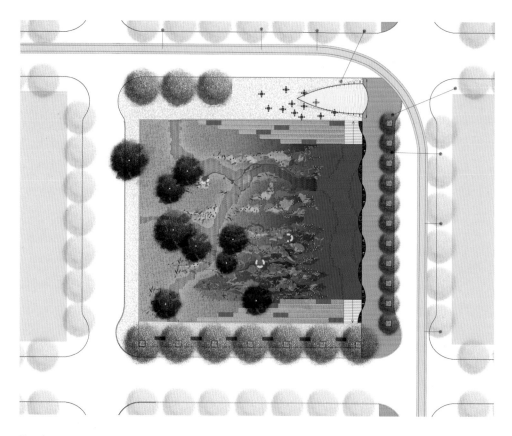

Site plan

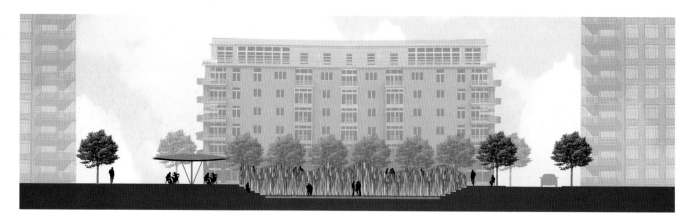

Park elevation at daytime

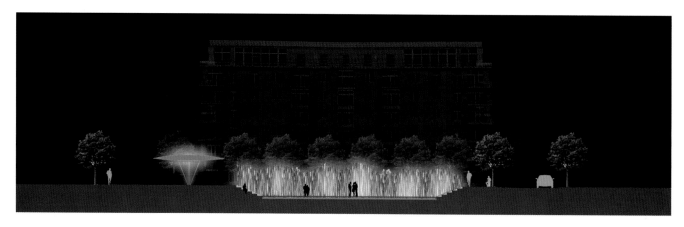

Park elevation at nighttime

# SENSATIONAL GARDEN

## Frosinone, Italy   2011

The sensational garden is part of a master plan intended to integrate public spaces into a residential neighborhood that was rapidly degrading. The project consists of an interactive garden with features that stimulate the five senses: sight, hearing, taste, smell, and touch. In that way, the park is an invitation to discover different views of the garden through paths around large conical protrusions. These protrusions, which incorporate planting beds, playgrounds, and sitting areas, obstruct any general view of the garden. By reducing the sense of direction, all of the other senses are enhanced, making visitors more aware of the space around them, as well as of their body movement. Sight is attracted by the beautiful rose garden; hearing, from the amplification of the sounds of wild game; taste is stimulated by the fruit trees; smell is attracted by flower scent; and touch, from feeling the materials of the central cone.

The balanced mix of natural elements (trees, shrubs, and flowers) and artificial materials (cement and resin) make the garden an environment that is durable and mutable.

**ARCHITECT**
Nabito Architects

**LOCATION**
Frosinone, Italy

**CLIENT**
Municipality of Frosinone

**COLLABORATORS**
Davide Fois, Lucio Altana, Joanna Rodriguez Noyola, Agita Putnina, Furio Sordini; EDILCM (contractor).

**AREA**
32,291 sq ft (3000 m²)

**COST**
n/a

**PHOTOGRAPHER**
Nabito Architects

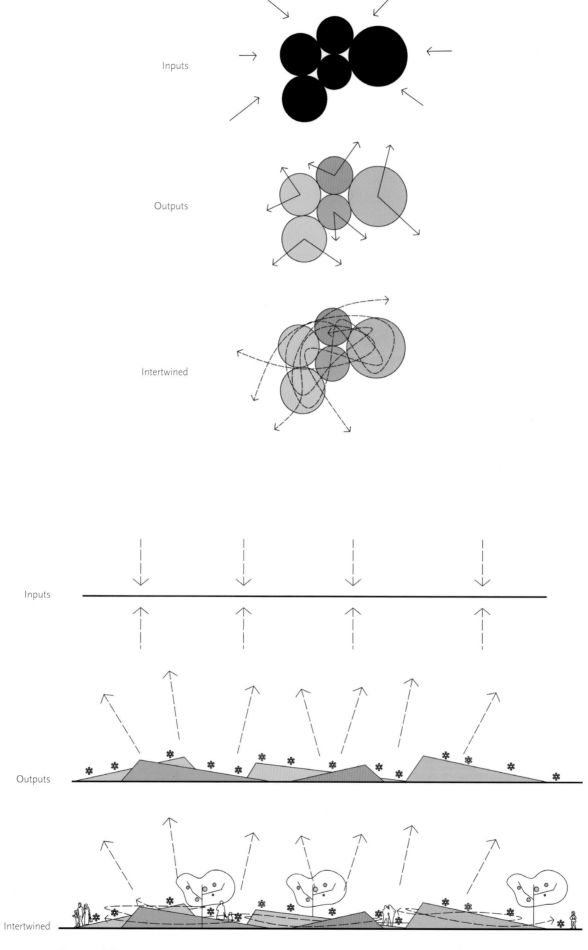

Inputs

Outputs

Intertwined

Inputs

Outputs

Intertwined

Conceptual diagrams

Visitors have no complete view of the garden. This design strategy forces people to be more aware of their immediate surroundings. The recreational aspect of the garden is reinforced by the conical shapes, which invite physical interaction.

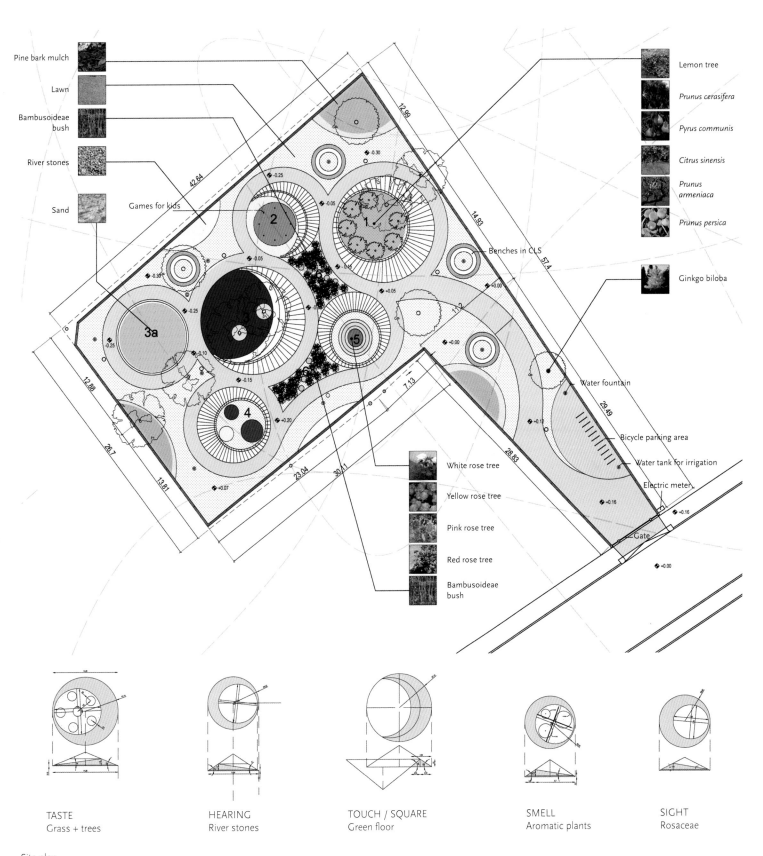

Pine bark mulch

Lawn

Bambusoideae bush

River stones

Sand

Games for kids

Lemon tree

Prunus cerasifera

Pyrus communis

Citrus sinensis

Prunus armeniaca

Prunus persica

Ginkgo biloba

Benches in CLS

Water fountain

Bicycle parking area

Water tank for irrigation

Electric meter

Gate

White rose tree

Yellow rose tree

Pink rose tree

Red rose tree

Bambusoideae bush

TASTE
Grass + trees

HEARING
River stones

TOUCH / SQUARE
Green floor

SMELL
Aromatic plants

SIGHT
Rosaceae

Site plan

Visitors are confronted with scenery that stimulates human senses in terms of materials, colors, aromas, and sounds. The garden is designed to be discovered little by little, so as to encourage visitors to continue their sensorial experience.

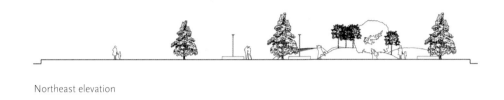

Sections

Northeast elevation

Southeast elevation

PARCO DEI MORE

# GENERAL MASTER PLAN
# FOR THE SILEA URBAN PARK

## Silea, Italy    (ongoing)

The reorganization of Parco dei Moreri takes place through the reconfiguration of the existing areas and the introduction of new ones to expand the variety of cultural and recreational activities available to include jogging, skating, playing, reading, climbing, strolling, talking, listening, sitting, and so on.

The first and only built phase of the project focuses on safety and accessibility issues that affect pedestrians, bicyclists, and motorized vehicles. Signage is an important design element, fulfilling its function to inform but also organizing the different spaces to create areas of focus.

The main route is represented by a long, colored concrete path that connects the different sections of the park. Its capacity for expansion beyond the boundaries of the park makes it a potential organizational element of Silea's urban fabric. A secondary path made of rubber connects the areas occupied by playgrounds. The playful and creative character of these areas is reinforced by the bubbling of the pavement into small mounds. Finally, the grassy fields planted with white mulberry trees are a reference to the agriculture that characterizes the landscape of the area.

**ARCHITECT**
made associati_ architettura e paesaggio

**CLIENT**
Comune di Silea

**COLLABORATORS**
Monica Martini

**AREA**
538,195 sq ft (50,000 m²)

**COST**
USD 109 million (EUR 80,000,000) (first phase)

**PHOTOGRAPHER**
Adriano Marangon

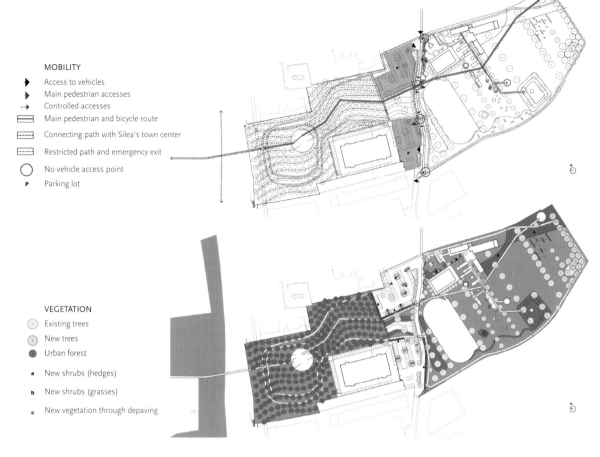

## MOBILITY

▸ Access to vehicles
▸ Main pedestrian accesses
⇢ Controlled accesses
▱ Main pedestrian and bicycle route
┄ Connecting path with Silea's town center
┈ Restricted path and emergency exit
◯ No vehicle access point
**P** Parking lot

## VEGETATION

⊙ Existing trees
⊙ New trees
● Urban forest

**a** New shrubs (hedges)
**b** New shrubs (grasses)
**c** New vegetation through depaving

Circulation and vegetation plan of the park

## HEDGE

General scheme

Section

Common hawthorn / *Crataegus monogyna*

Wild blackberry / *Rubus ulmifolius*

## COLORED CONCRETE BLOCKS

General scheme

Pedestrian and bicycle path

Passage too narrow for motorcycles

Wheelchair passage

Path with double curvature prevents motorcycles from passing

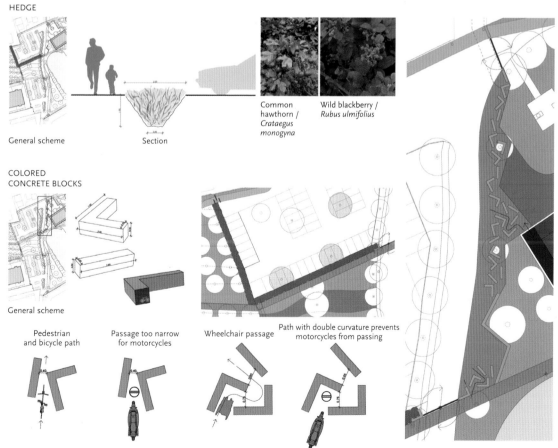

Diagram of the compositional elements of the park

# THE DOLL

Allariz, Spain   2011

The Doll is a project by the French Office of Architecture and landscape architecture firm Oglo. The design was selected by the Municipality of Allariz, Spain, to be built for the 2011 Allariz Garden Festival with the theme "Fashion in the garden." The colorful design makes reference to the industrial textile past of this old village of the Galicia province.

The essence of fashion finds its roots in the characteristics of the human body, regardless of the culture it is a part of or the time and place it refers to. Dimensions and proportions are critical design elements to enhance the body. Static and still when unworn, fashion transforms itself in space when inhabited. Once wrapped around the being, fashion—lifeless until then— comes alive.

After going past a diaphanous plant screen, a narrow path with soft curves guides the visitor through a world of scents and colors produced by a rich variety of flowers. At the end of the spiraling path, visitors rest, impervious under the colorful skirt of a seemingly gyrating body.

**ARCHITECT**
Oglo

**CLIENT**
Concello de Allariz

**AREA**
2,153 sq ft (200 m²)

**COST**
USD 13,617 (EUR 10,000)

**PHOTOGRAPHER**
Oglo (Emmanuel de France & Arnaud Dambrine)

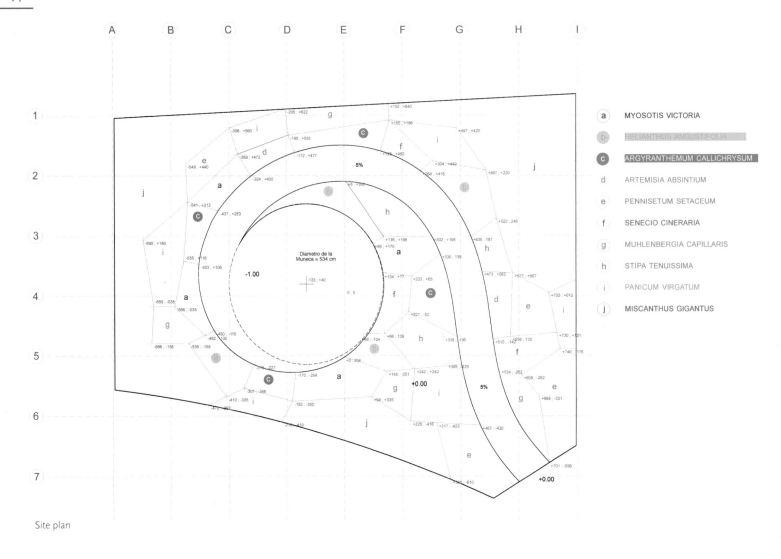

a  MYOSOTIS VICTORIA

b  HELIANTHUS ANGUSTIFOLIA

c  ARGYRANTHEMUM CALLICHRYSUM

d  ARTEMISIA ABSINTIUM

e  PENNISETUM SETACEUM

f  SENECIO CINERARIA

g  MUHLENBERGIA CAPILLARIS

h  STIPA TENUISSIMA

i  PANICUM VIRGATUM

j  MISCANTHUS GIGANTUS

Site plan

Section

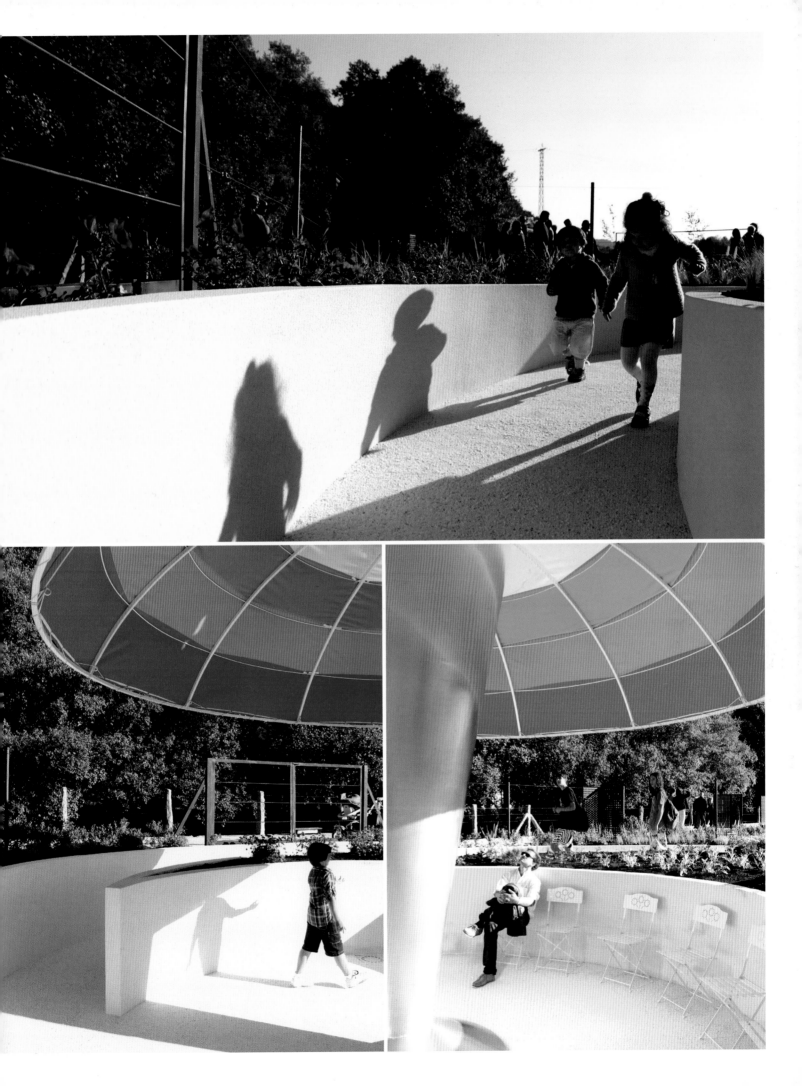

# ECO-BOULEVARD IN VALLECAS

Madrid, Spain  2007

The eco-boulevard is an innovative project fostered by the City of Madrid for a new residential area. It consists of three aligned large cylinders intended to vivify an existing boulevard with few interesting qualities. These cylinders function as trees, capable of changing the levels of humidity and air of the area they occupy. Made from 90 percent recycled materials, including rubber, steel, and concrete, these "air trees" produce electricity through solar panels installed on their tops. Like trees, the cylinders help regenerate and purify up to eleven tons of polluting gases annually. They are not built to remain permanently; instead, they will be removed when the real trees, still young, reach a reasonably large size and become able to fulfill their environmental functions. In the meantime, the cylinders invite interaction, turning a desolate boulevard into a meeting place for neighbors and visitors.

**ARCHITECT**
Ecosistema Urbano

**LOCATION**
Madrid, Spain

**CLIENT**
Empresa Municipal de Vivienda y Suelo, Ayuntamiento de Madrid, Dirección de Proyectos de Innovación Residencial

**COLLABORATORS**
Structure: Tectum Ingeniería, S.L. (Constantino Hurtado); Construction: Grupo Entorno, S.A., Utilities: IP Ingeniería; Landscape: Ignacio López

**AREA**
296,000 sq ft (27,500 m²)

**COST**
n/a

**AWARD**
2007 Emerging Award
from *Architectural Review*

**PHOTOGRAPHER**
Emilio P. Doiztua and Roland Halbe

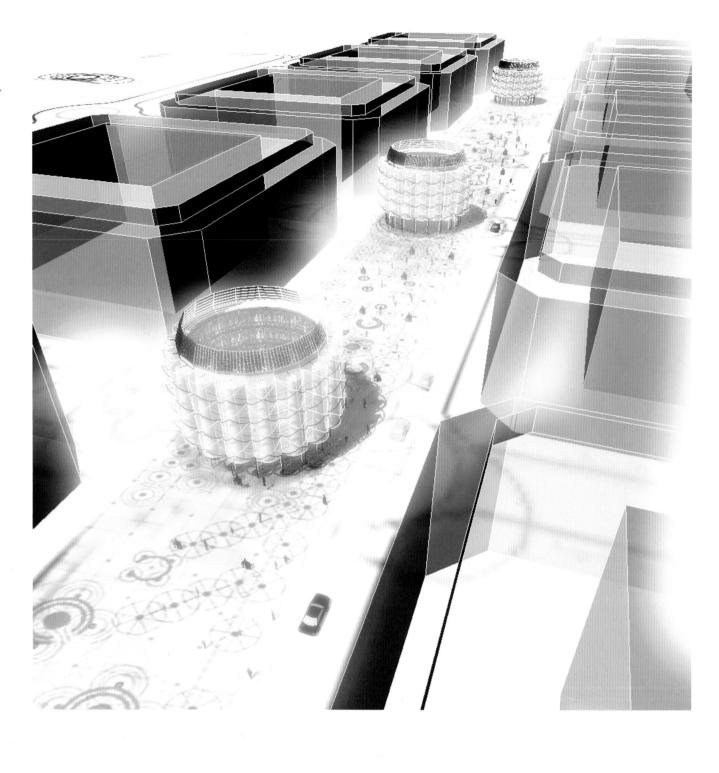

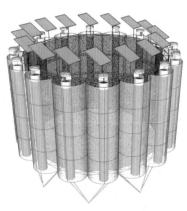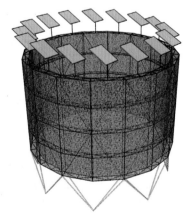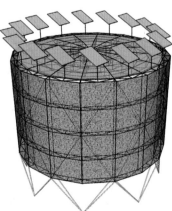

Perspective views of the "air trees"

he "air trees" are lightweight steel structures
nstalled on a rubber pavement. They are easy to build
nd disassemble and self-sufficient in terms of energy.

The environmental character of the design lies in the use of recycled materials, renewable energy, and a passive cooling system. The "air trees" promote social interaction, and their disposition organizes traffic at the intersections.

Once the planted trees have reached maturity and can fulfill their environmental functions, the "air trees" will be taken apart and transported to another part of the country where they can be of use.

# PROMENADE OF LIGHT

## London, United Kingdom  2007

Promenade of Light is the renewal project for the pedestrian area west of Old Street London. Previously a neglected part of the city at the gates of the financial district, this area has become a vital public space that is safer and fully accessible. From the start, the project has been an exemplary case of collaboration between the design team and the local community. Users have expressed that they feel safer on the promenade and that the improved streetscape has benefited local businesses.

Recognizing the broad demographic of users and the different patterns and paces of their occupations, Tonkin Liu has created a space that unifies the diverse activity of the street and slows down the pace of its users.

Retaining the twenty-one mature plane trees, the new promenade features an additional eighteen specimens to delineate two distinct rows. An underused grassed area at the center of the site has been paved in granite, making it fully accessible and better able to accommodate the flow of commuters during rush hour. Every tree in the scheme has been treated with a ring, which takes the form of a bench, a table, a planter, or cycle facilities. Rings for people are benches and tables; rings for plants are filled with brightly colored flowers.

**ARCHITECT**
Tonkin Liu

**LOCATION**
London, United Kingdom

**CLIENT**
Islington Council

**COLLABORATORS**
Atelier One (structural engineering), Traffic and Engineering, Transport Planning and Environment & Conservation units of London Borough of Islington.

**AREA**
n/a

**COST**
USD 1,563,650 (£1 million)

**AWARDS**
First place in the Royal Institute of British Architects (RIBA) Urban Space by Design (unbuilt category) competition; 2007 RIBA award

**PHOTOGRAPHER**
Keith Collie

The scheme resurrects the charming tree-lined promenade of the eighteenth and nineteenth centuries, an arrangement complemented with a series of lamp columns that make the promenade safer and more attractive at night.

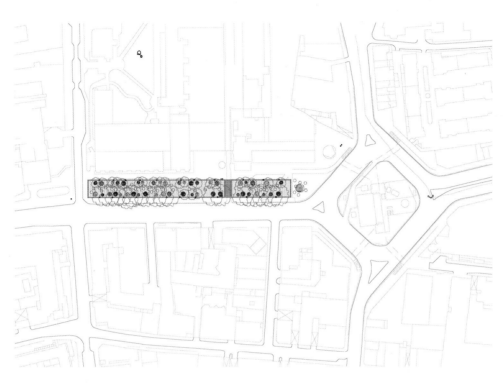

Site plan

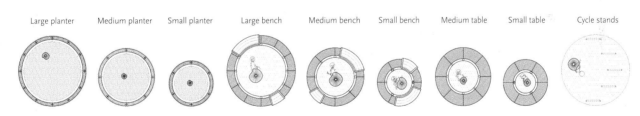

| Large planter | Medium planter | Small planter | Large bench | Medium bench | Small bench | Medium table | Small table | Cycle stands |

Key chart of rings

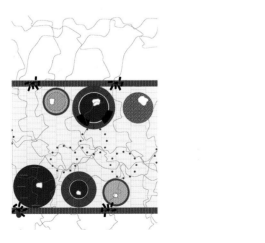

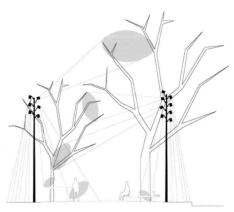

Partial enlarged plan and cross section through promenade

# SØNDER BOULEVARD

## Copenhagen, Denmark   2007

Sønder Boulevard cuts through Copenhagen's inner city quarter, Vesterbro, as a vestige of the nineteenth-century dream for a great metropolis. Over the years, traffic-ridden roads, barren infrastructures, and unmaintained grass patches took over the once-proud boulevard. SLA was commissioned to revitalize and adjust Sønder Boulevard to the city's present needs. Through a comprehensive community participation process, the residents of the area had the opportunity to put their fingerprint on this urban space in the form of recreational zones, seating areas, paths, and small, peaceful gardens.

SLA developed a proposal for the framework, while the residents determined which activities and uses should be incorporated. This collaboration resulted in spaces for everybody's use and valuable amenities for the whole community.
A simple arrangement of the central space with rows of different tree species along the entire boulevard provides variation, but also allows future uses to be incorporated into the plan. The trees were chosen for their color, changing foliage through the seasons. Thus the boulevard is always experienced in different ways and draws the beauty of nature right into the inner city.

**LANDSCAPE ARCHITECT**
SLA

**CLIENT**
Municipality of Copenhagen

**COLLABORATORS**
Hansen & Henneberg (environment and safety consultants)

**AREA**
3.95 acres (1.6 ha)

**COST**
USD 3,270,240 million (EUR 2.4 million)

**AWARDS**
2008 European Prize for Urban Public Spaces from the Center of Contemporary Culture of Barcelona (CCCB)

**PHOTOGRAPHER**
SLA

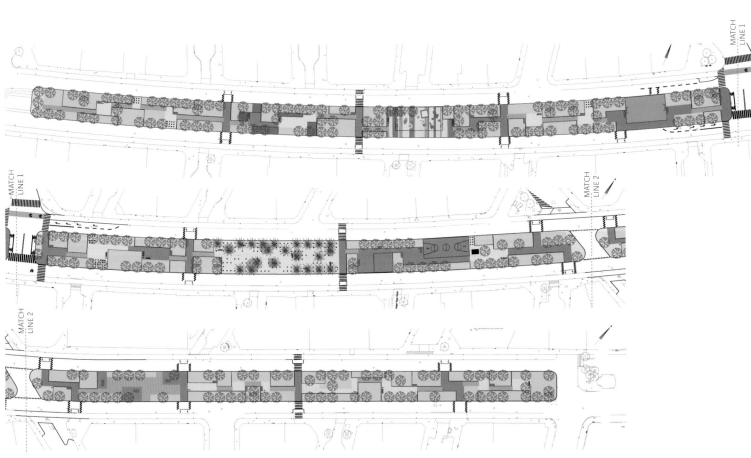

Site plan

The narrowing of the roads along Sønder Boulevard
means two things: traffic has slowed down and
the linear recreational space down the center of
the boulevard is wider, allowing for the creation of
basketball courts, playgrounds, and benches.

# BREITEWEG

## Barleben, Germany   2009

Located 100 km southwest of Berlin, Barleben has a historic urban fabric that includes a marketplace as a meeting point and central event space for the town. The renovation of the so-called Breiteweg sets a benchmark in terms of urban quality, while the creative and original design reveals the spirit of this active small town.

Eight light and water sculptures are grouped irregularly in four clusters along the 750 m streetscape to create a dynamic field of connectivity.

The Breiteweg has become popular with young and old people, who come there to play, walk, and meet friends. More than an urban playground or illuminated fountain, these art installations have made the Breiteweg a very special place, the self-confident and daring character of which set a cultural impulse for the future.

**LANDSCAPE ARCHITECT**
Atelier Dreiseitl

**CLIENT**
City of Barleben

**COLLABORATORS**
Pro Plan

**AREA**
3,230 sq ft (300 m²)

**COST**
n/a

**PHOTOGRAPHER**
Atelier Dreiseitl

Steel mesh netting is stretched to draw a sheet of water down to the ground. At night, this water sheet is illuminated from above, transforming the ground into a water and light wave that flows along the length of the streetscape.

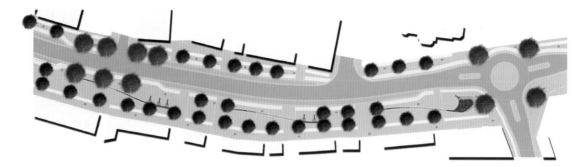

Site plan

Section at daytime

Section at nighttime

# BATTERY PARK CITY STREETSCAPE

## New York, NY, USA    2006

The Battery Park City Streetscape project encompasses a large area and has several overlapping programs and planned uses. It affects two medians on North End Avenue between Teardrop Park and the Battery Park City ball fields, and Vesey Street between the Hudson River and the World Trade Center complex.

The medians form a linear park that includes a dog run park, a nursery, and a more open green space at the north end of the development. The design links together these green medians and their programs with a series of shade structures.

Light is a critical element of the design to reinforce the linear nature of this path, facilitating both the pedestrian and vehicular circulation of this area while establishing a security barrier that protects the financial institutions immediately to the south. This security barrier is concealed below the walking surface and within an illuminated cast glass base, establishing a visually delicate barrier that reflects the activity during the day and emits subtle light at night. This strategy activates life on the street without interrupting everyday circulation patterns.

**DESIGNERS**
Rogers Marvel Architects with James Carpenter Design Associates

**CLIENT**
Battery Park City Authority

**COLLABORATORS**
Robert Silman Associates (structural engineers)

**AREA**
Phase I: North Neighborhood 54,000 sq ft; WTC Streetscapes 84,000 sq ft

**COST**
USD 26.5 million

**AWARDS**
2007 Project merit Award from the American Institute of Architects (AIA) New York Chapter; 2005 National Urban Design Award from the American Institute of Architects; 2005 National Analysis and Planning Award from the American Society of Landscape Architects (ASLA)

**PHOTOGRAPHER**
Andreas Keller

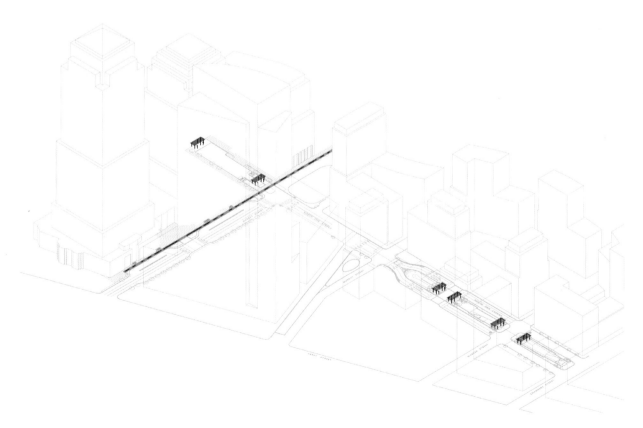

Axonometric view of the Battery Park City streetscape

he prismatic cast glass of the benches creates
solid volume of light in daylight and from
ternal illumination at night, improving
edestrian connections and building security.

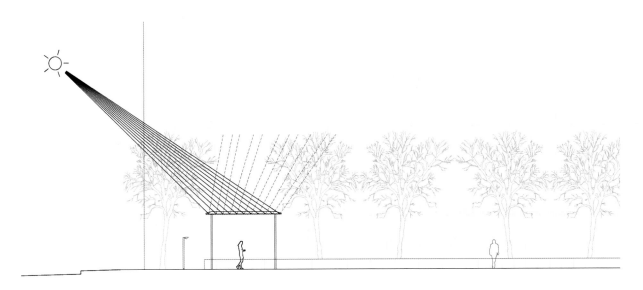

Detail of the canopy during the day

Detail of the canopy at nightime

The insertion of long expanses of light emphasizes
the linearity of the axis. The canopies direct a
soft light down to the ground during the day and,
due to a reflective interlayer, shine artificial light
beamed from below back down to the ground.

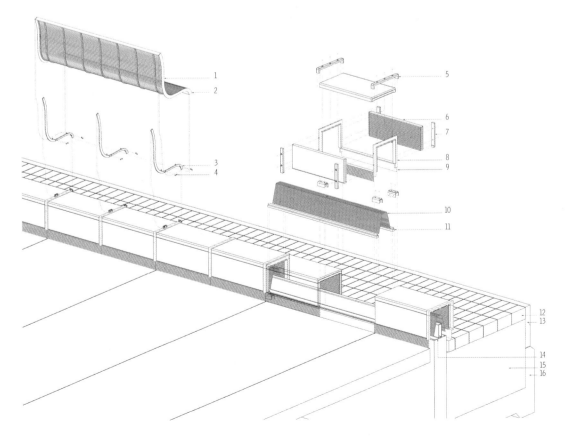

1. SST seat system, tri-wire welded to support ribs
2. Water-jet cut SST closure bar
3. Water-jet cut SST support bars
4. SST mechanical fastener system
5. SST closure rib, #6 finish, mechanically fastened to armature
6. Ribbed low expansion soda lime cast glass system
7. SST vert. closure rib, #6 finish, mechanically fastened to armature
8. SST armature mill finish
9. Ribbed SST reflective panel assembly
10. Ribbed SST reflective panel
11. Linear lighting system
12. Cobble stone
13. Stone curb
14. Concrete and steel security structure below
15. Collapsible fill
16. Concrete

Detail and overall view of the cast glass benches

# TKTS BOOTH & REDEVELOPMENT OF FATHER DUFFY SQUARE

New York, NY, USA    2008

This project started with an international competition to replace the existing TKTS booth in Times Square. The architectural team went beyond the competition's request for a small architectural structure and developed a plan for an urban redefinition. The conceptual approach responds to the designers thinking of Times Square as one of New York's great gathering points; and yet, there was nowhere for people to sit. The resulting design consists of a grand staircase of red resin that serves at the same time as the backdrop for the nearby statue of Father Duffy, and as the roof of the new TKTS booth. The twenty-seven-step red resin structure, shaped to reflect the footprint of Times Square, becomes a powerful landmark, especially at night when the staircase, lit from below, glows. This feature reinforces the presence and identity of the TKTS booth, while turning it into a strong marker in Times Square. The design has quickly become an important part of the city's popular culture and has been featured in the Will Smith film *I Am Legend* and in Jay-Z and Alicia Keys's music video for the song "Empire State of Mind".

**DESIGNERS**
Choi Ropiha, Perkins Eastman, PKSB Architects

**CLIENT**
Theatre development Fund, Time Square Alliance, Coalition for Father Duffy, The City of New York

**COLLABORATORS**
Dewhurst Macfarlane and Partners, Fisher Marantz Stone, Schaefer Lewis Engineers, DMJM Harris; Building contractor: Gorton Associates, D. Haller, Haran Glass with IG Innovation Glass, Merrifield Roberts

**AREA**
17,975 sq ft (entire plaza), 3,229 sq ft (booth and steps)

**COST**
n/a

**AWARDS**
2009 World Architecture Festival winner

**PHOTOGRAPHER**
John Saeyong Ra, Ari Burling, Choi Ropiha Fighera

While strengthening the presence of TKTS
in the visually charged Times Square, the
structure forms a new public space where
visitors and TKTS's clients can pause to sit and
absorb the cacophony of light and sound.

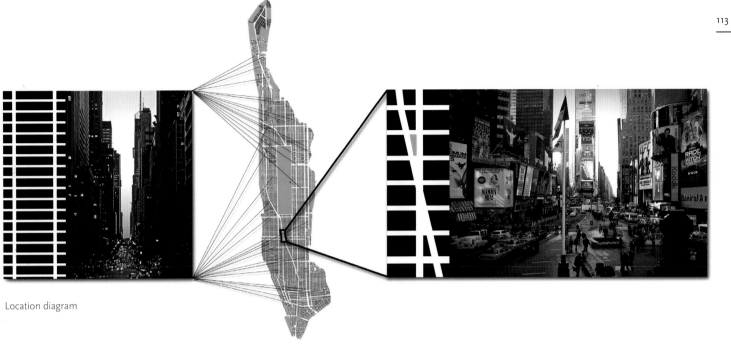

Location diagram

Elevations

Platform    Primary frame    Cladding    Red resin planks

Structure diagrams

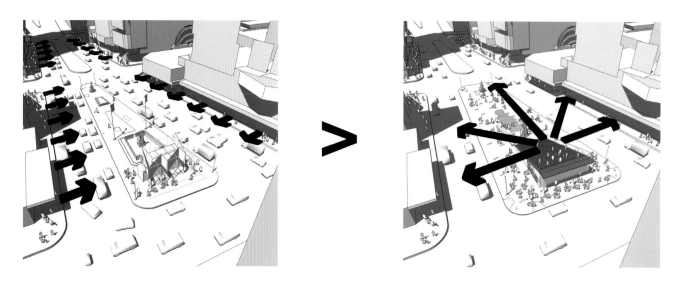

Diagram of the new structure's urban role

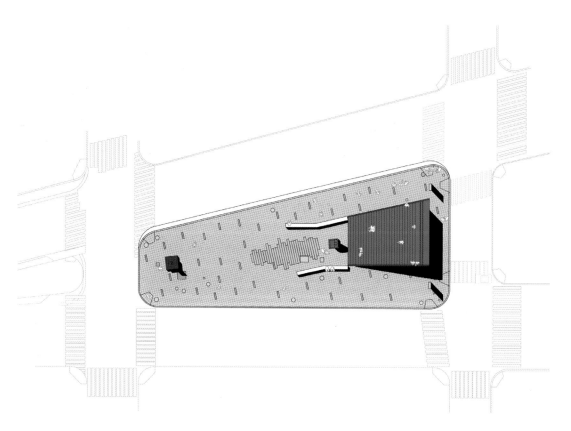

Site plan

king shelter under the resin steps is a freestanding
berglass structure that consists of twelve brightly
ticket windows. The new TKTS booth replaced
e structure that was built in 1973 and quickly
ecame a staple of New York's Times Square.

# SQUARE DES FRÈRES-CHARON

Montréal, Canada   2008

The Square of Frères-Charon is located at the crossroads of two historic streets in one of the oldest neighborhoods of Montreal. Affleck + de la Riva were part of a multidisciplinary design team that included the artist Raphaëlle de Groot and the landscape architect Robert Desjardins. The design, which consists of a series of circular and cylindrical forms, creates a dialogue between a garden of wild grasses, a paved strip, the vestiges of the foundations of a windmill from the French Colonial period, and a pavilion in the form of a park folly. This composition is rounded off with a lighting concept developed by Gilles Arpin that suggests a color-changing lighting scheme in accordance with the seasons.

The design focused on the experience of the contemporary city and urban lifestyles. This allowed the design team to explore concepts from a user's point of view and initiate a connection with the immediate surroundings. Square des Frères-Charon was carefully designed to ensure it is comfortable, safe, and wheelchair accessible. With its planted area, the square is an experience in contrast and connection with the surrounding city, while raising public awareness of the history and geography of the site.

**LANDSCAPE ARCHITECT**
Affleck + de la Riva architectes

**CLIENT**
City of Montreal, Large park management division

**COLLABORATORS**
Design: Robert des Jardins (landscape), Raphaëlle de Groot Arts, Éclairage (public Lighting), Sandra Baronne (horticulture), Morelli Designers (industrial design), Moitiémoitié exposition (museology), Genivar (structural, mechanical, electrical, civil) construction); construction: Quartier International de Montréal (construction management), Terramex (landscape) Celeb (pavilion)

**AREA**
17,650 sq ft (1,640 m²)

**COST**
USD 2,134,844 (Can$ 2,200,000)

**PHOTOGRAPHER**
Marc Cramer

Built as a response to the urban revitalization of a disaffected industrial sector, Square des Frères-Charon is an entirely new public amenity in a space that is more than 150 years old. The new square provides identity, civic pride, and generous outdoor areas for year-round public use.

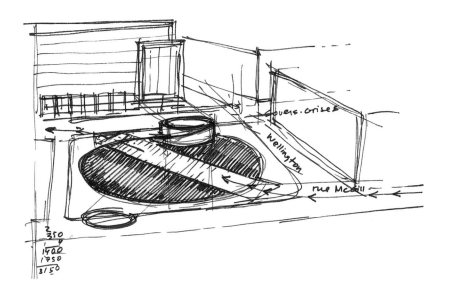

Square des Frères Charon offers the experience of a contemporary urban landscape inspired by the original vocation of the site, a prairie wetland where the Charon brothers built a windmill in the seventeenth century.

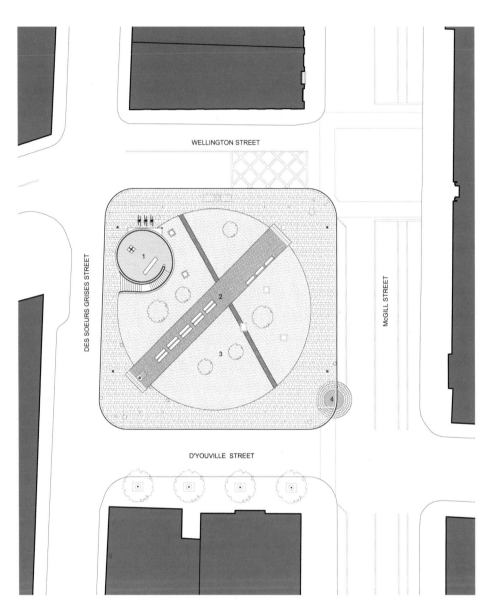

Site plan

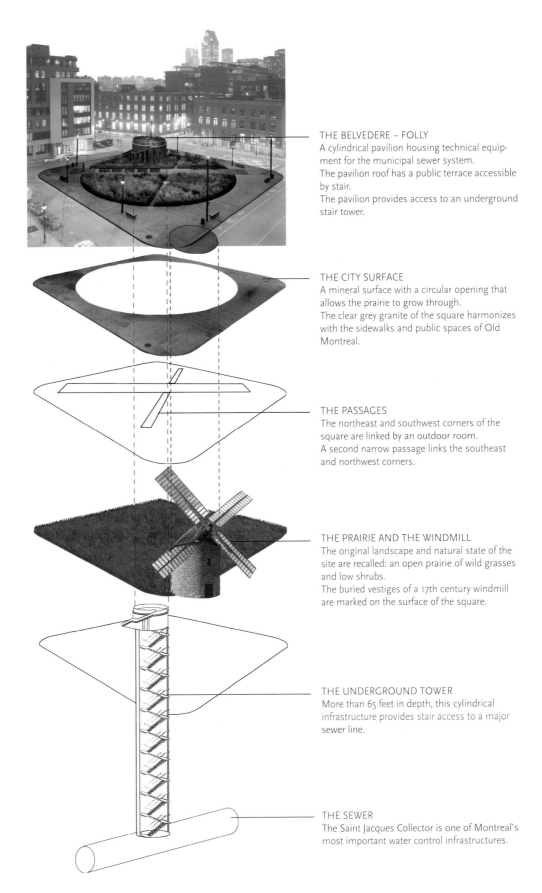

**THE BELVEDERE – FOLLY**
A cylindrical pavilion housing technical equipment for the municipal sewer system.
The pavilion roof has a public terrace accessible by stair.
The pavilion provides access to an underground stair tower.

**THE CITY SURFACE**
A mineral surface with a circular opening that allows the prairie to grow through.
The clear grey granite of the square harmonizes with the sidewalks and public spaces of Old Montreal.

**THE PASSAGES**
The northeast and southwest corners of the square are linked by an outdoor room.
A second narrow passage links the southeast and northwest corners.

**THE PRAIRIE AND THE WINDMILL**
The original landscape and natural state of the site are recalled: an open prairie of wild grasses and low shrubs.
The buried vestiges of a 17th century windmill are marked on the surface of the square.

**THE UNDERGROUND TOWER**
More than 65 feet in depth, this cylindrical infrastructure provides stair access to a major sewer line.

**THE SEWER**
The Saint Jacques Collector is one of Montreal's most important water control infrastructures.

Schematic design of the square

Sustainable initiatives include the planting of local species of wild grasses, which take a significant load off the municipal irrigation system, the use of durable Quebec granite for hard landscaping, and the cladding of the park pavilion.

# FRIEDRICH-EBERT-PLATZ

Heidelberg, Germany   2010

Friedrich-Ebert Square forms a compact urban space, which is reactivated by simple materials and strong spatial vocabulary. The revitalization of the town square and market is made possible by the basic idea to exempt the inner space in order to create a simple and functional spatial layout. The rows of trees along the west and east sides direct the view to the hillside areas of the Odenwald forest at the south. To gain an open view of the square, the bus stop is oriented toward the north-south direction on the southern end of the square. A gray quartzite sandstone is used to obtain a homogeneous surface throughout the site. The sidewalks of the surrounding streets are paved with the same material to give the impression of a connection with the facades of the buildings. The ramps to and from the underground parking garage are located at the southern part of the square, close to the site. The ramp surfaces are made out of asphalt integrated into the color scheme.

**LANDSCAPE ARCHITECT**
Topotek 1

**CLIENT**
City of Heidelberg

**COLLABORATORS**
ap 88

**AREA**
37,673 sq ft (3.500 m²)

**COST**
USD 1,660,000 (EUR 1,300,000)

**PHOTOGRAPHER**
Topotek 1

The rows of trees and benches accentuate the long and narrow proportions of the plaza and intensify the perspective effect toward the Odenwald forest while screening the underground garage entry and exit ramps.

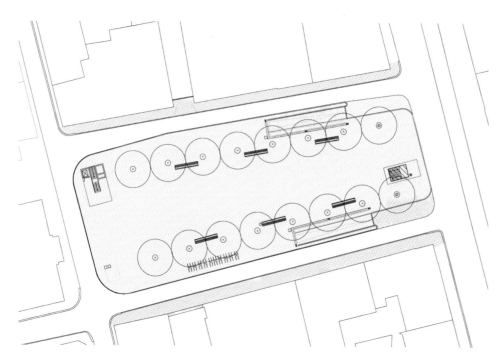

Site plan

# "LA CRAQUELURE." RESTORATION
# OF MATTEOTTI SQUARE

## Badalucco, Italy    2008

*Craquelure* is the French word for crack and is the theme of this project for a square that features a pavement that, because of its design, color, and material, is reminiscent of mud dried in the sun. The square is a long and narrow area enclosed by four-story-tall buildings on three sides. It slopes down toward the fourth side, which is open to the main road and to the valley with a river and olive groves.

The layout of the square is based on the idea of transferring the vertical plane formed by the row of buildings on the two long sides onto the horizontal plane. This results in the subdivision of the square's pavement representing the outline of the buildings. The simple plan makes reference to the narrow streets and roofs of the old buildings in this small town of the Liguria region. At a different level, the buildings cast their shadows onto the fragmented pavement, adding three-dimensionality. To reinforce this sense of depth, the benches and planting beds are laid out horizontally in contrast with the slight slope of the square. The olive trees soften the rigid grid of the pavement while alluding to the essence of the Mediterranean region.

**ARCHITECT**
mag.MA architetture

**LOCATION**
Badalucco, Italy

**CLIENT**
Municipality of Badalucco

**COLLABORATORS**
Masala (building contractor)

**AREA**
7,000 sq ft (650 m²)

**COST**
USD 143,657 (EUR 112,500)

**PHOTOGRAPHER**
mag.MA architetture

Section A-A

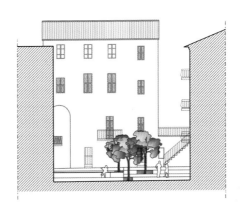

Section B-B

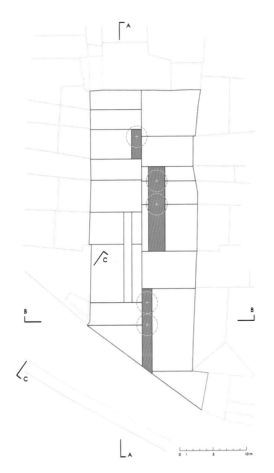

Site plan of Matteotti Square

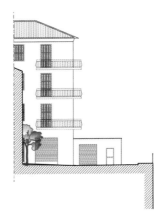

Section C-C

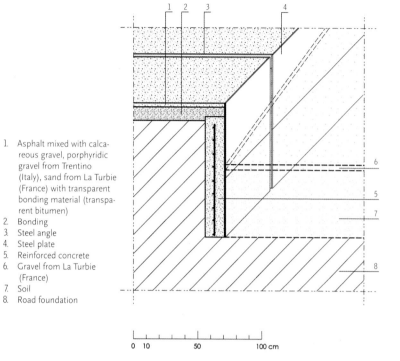

1. Asphalt mixed with calcareous gravel, porphyridic
   gravel from Trentino
   (Italy), sand from La Turbie
   (France) with transparent
   bonding material (transparent bitumen)
2. Bonding
3. Steel angle
4. Steel plate
5. Reinforced concrete
6. Gravel from La Turbie
   (France)
7. Soil
8. Road foundation

0  10        50        100 cm

Flower-bed, detail

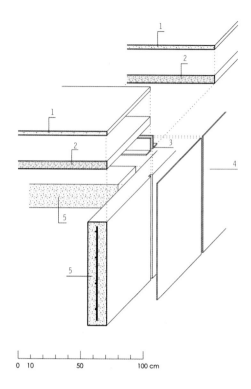

0  10        50        100 cm

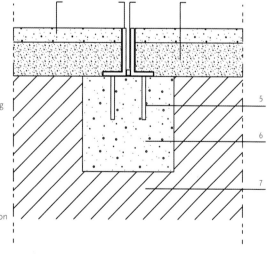

1. Asphalt mixed with
   calcareous gravel,
   porphyridic gravel from
   Trentino (Italy), sand
   from La Turbie (France)
   with transparent bonding
   material (transparent
   bitumen)
2. Bonding
3. Steel angle
4. Light
5. Metal anchor
6. Reinforced concrete
   foundation
7. Road foundation
8. Bench detail, cross-section

Flooring detail, section

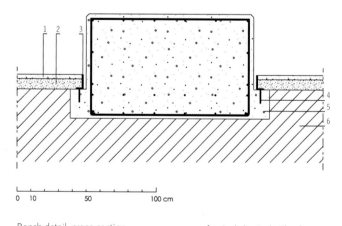

0  10        50        100 cm

Bench detail, cross-section

1. Asphalt mixed with calcareous
   gravel, porphyridic gravel
   from Trentino (Italy), sand
   from La Turbie (France) with
   transparent bonding material
   (transparent bitumen)
2. Bonding
3. Steel angle
4. Metal anchor
5. Reinforced
6. Road foundation

The sense of depth is even more visible from the road. From there, the inclination of the pavement increases the effect of the perspective; a technique used in theater where stages are tilted from front to back to contribute to the illusion of perspective.

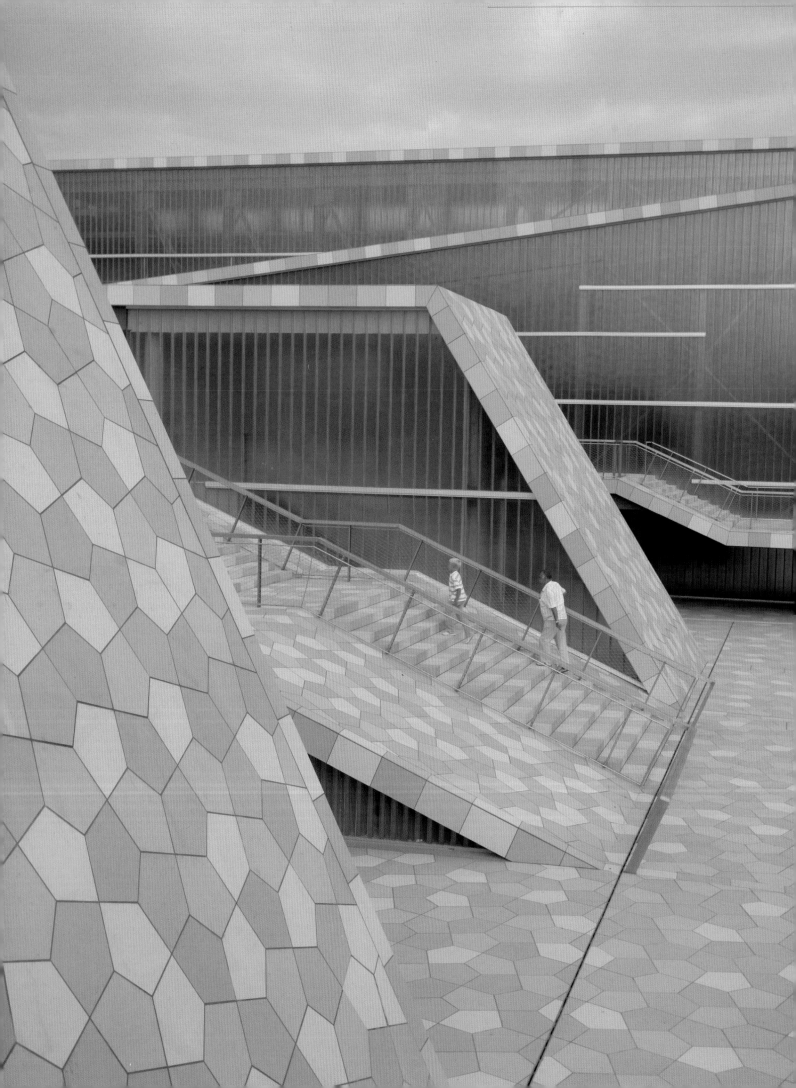

# ZAMET CENTER

Rijeka, Croatia    2009

The Zamet Center accommodates various facilities, including a sports hall, a local community office, a city library, thirteen commercial spaces, and a parking garage. Except for a third of the sports hall that is built into the ground, the public facilities fit entirely into the above ground surroundings. Given its striking form, the center redefines the urban context, making an impact on the otherwise bland urban and architectural setting. Its strong presence generates a landmark and reshapes the topography. Beyond being just another building in town, the center is a powerful urban element.

The main architectural characteristic of the Zamet Center are "ribbons" stretching in a north-south direction. They function simultaneously as an architectural design element and as a zoning feature, which forms a public square and a link between a park and a school on the north and a major street on the south. The roof of the center integrates a public space that acts as an extension of the park. The goal of the project was to create a new space for the inhabitants of Zamet's quarter to use as an outdoor space for their recreational and social activities.

**ARCHITECT**
3LHD

**CLIENT**
Grad Rijeka / Rijeka Sport

**COLLABORATORS**
Mateo Bilus, Building Physics / Details; Berislav Medic, UPI-2M, Structural Engineering; Branko Čorko, IPZ-elektroinzenjering 22, Electrical Engineering; Mario Lukenda, Termoinzenjering-projektiranje, HVAC; Slavko Simunović, HIT PROJEKT, MEP Engineering - Plumbing; Nenad Semenov, PASTOR, sprinkler installation; Rok Pietri, LIFT MODUS, elevators; Zeljko Arbanas, IGH PC Rijeka, diaphragm wall; Zeljko Stipković, Fire Protection; Ivica Babic, Zavod za zastitu na radu Rijeka, Safety at Work; Marija Babojelic, Special Consultant – Cost Consultant; Ines Hrdalo, Landscape Architect; Damir Bralić, Lana Cavar i Narcisa Vukojevic, signage and environmental graphics design; Nikola Durek, "Typonine Zamet" typeface design; Main contractor: GP Krk

**AREA**
181,156 sq ft (16830 m²) (site area)

**COST**
USD 27,252 (EUR 20,000)

**PHOTOGRAPHER**
Domagoj Blazevic, Damir Fabijanic, 3LHD

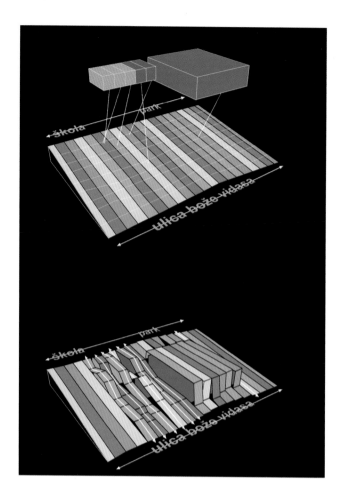

Conceptual diagram

1.  Square
2.  Utility court
3.  Entrance for visitors
4.  Entrance for players
5.  Entrance for press
6.  Entrance for VIP
7.  Local community
8.  Library
9.  Entrance shops

Site plan

The challenge that this project implied laid in its
integration into the urban structure of Zamet.
In addition to the creation of new facilities for
the neighborhood, the center redefines the role
of this sector of the city as an important center
of pedestrian and vehicular circulation.

The ribbon-like stripes were inspired by "gromača,"
a type of rocks specific to Rijeka, which the center
artificially reinterprets by color and shape. Stripes
are covered with 51,000 ceramic tiles designed by
3LHD and manufactured specially for the center.

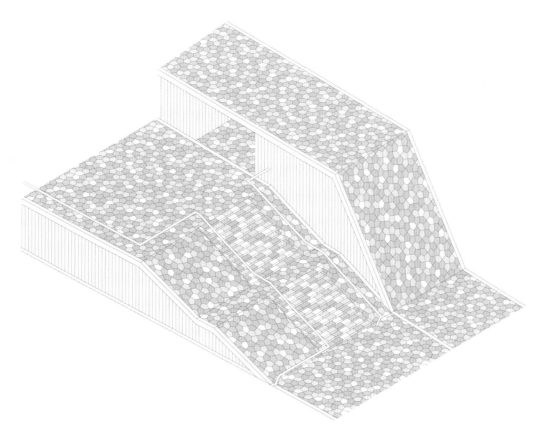

Axonometric detail of tile work

Centar Zamet
Investitor: Rijeka sport
Projektant: 3LHD
Izvođač: GP Krk
Nadzor: IGH / 3LHD
Rijeka, 2009.

# PUBLIC SPACES AROUND INSTITUTIONAL DEVELOPMENTS

|| barcode luminescence | mikyoung kim | 2008 | ocean county library ||

# BARCODE LUMINESCENCE

## Toms River, NJ, USA    2008

The plaza that fronts the Ocean County Public Library is located in the heart of the Toms River community. This nationally recognized library is both a traditional sited institution and a traveling library. The plaza, part of a new construction that connects with the historic building, integrates new technologies to convey information to the community. The design of this dynamic new entry plaza recognizes the well-traveled paths of the mobile institution and reflects the information patterns of the library in the digital age.

The project constitutes an open courtyard and establishes a sense of entry to the Ocean County Public Library. It also integrates public art by way of lantern sculptures that create dynamic and engaging spatial transitions within the plaza, while relating to the library's role within the community.

Wrapped in perforated stainless steel and dichroic resin panels, the barcode patterns of the lanterns represent the transmission of digital information. The pattern abstraction of the barcode language was translated onto stainless steel plates through laser cutting. The angles of the bar-coded design between the inner and outer spirals were aligned and calibrated to create an arresting moiré pattern.

**LANDSCAPE ARCHITECT**
Mikyoung Kim Design

**CLIENT**
Ocean County Public Library

**COST**
n/a

**PHOTOGRAPHER**
Marc La Rosa

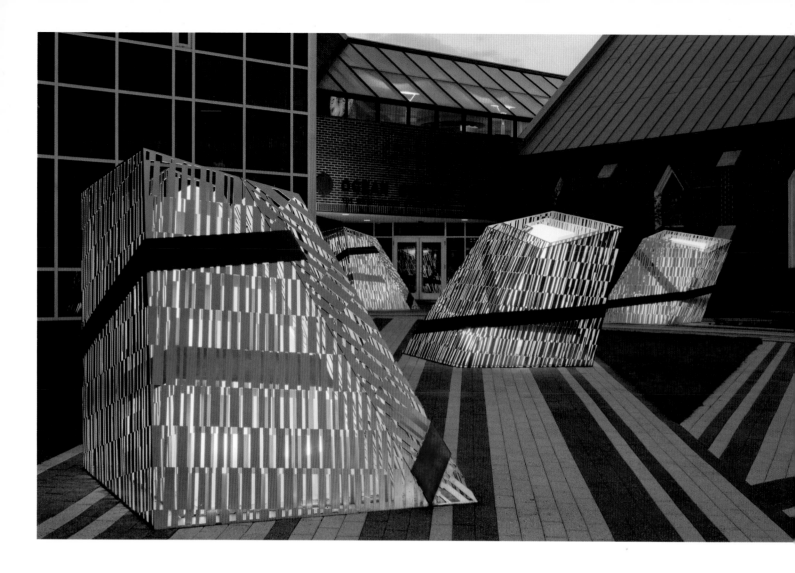

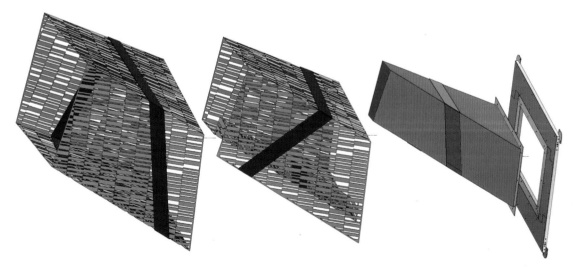

Diagram of the stainless steel and dichroic resin lantern sculptures

Middle ribbon:
120" × 8" SST, blackened finish
Plug welded to inner face of
outer spiral

Outer ribbon:
250" × 8" SST, blackened finish
Plug welded to outer face of
outer spiral

Outer spiral:
187" SST, non-directional finish
Laser cut geometric pattern

Inner ribbon:
120" × 8" SST, blackened finish
Plug welded to outer face of
inner spiral

Acrylic ribbon by others

Dichroic acrylic core by others

Base platform constructed of
aluminum channel and plate

e paving of crisscrossing paths reinforce
nnective relationships between the institution
d the community. Integrated with the paved
aza are lantern sculptures that illuminate the
ths at night, guiding visitors to the library.

# NICOLAI

## Kolding, Denmark    2007

Saint Nicholas had been a school since 1890, but over the years the schoolyard as well as all the buildings had deteriorated and become unfit for modern school life. Eventually the backyard was used as a parking lot surrounded by buildings in disrepair. The Municipality of Kolding and the Realdania Foundation commissioned a project that would transform the complex into a cultural center.

With its five art houses, Sct. Nicolai School Center offers new possibilities for an emerging typology of cultural institutions. The project evolved from the idea of the schoolyard as a center that ties the different functions together. The schoolyard offers outdoor activities linked to the different programs presented in the complex: cinema, literature, children's activities, craftsmanship, and music. Additionally, it accommodates thematic areas such as the Garden of Tales, the City Garden, the Market Square, and the Plaza.

The new black asphalt is a unifying surface that covers the entire schoolyard. Like a blackboard, it serves as support for dynamic drawings made of bright white thermoplastic paint that link the various buildings. A long Corten steel wall frames the courtyard and ties various buildings together. This material is also used to create architectural features in the courtyard, such as a small amphitheater.

**ARCHITECT**
Arkitekt Kristine Jensens Tegnestue

**LOCATION**
Kolding, Denmark

**CLIENT**
The Municipality of Kolding

**COLLABORATORS**
Dorte Mandrup Arkitekter

**AREA**
40,900 sq ft (3,800 m²)

**COST**
USD 1,361,700 (EUR 1 million)

**AWARDS**
First Prize in 5th European Biennial of Landscape Architecture (2008)

**PHOTOGRAPHER**
Bjarne Frost, Simon Høgsberg

The new schoolyard has become an interactive
place where children and adults can enjoy the
different activities offered by the cultural center
or simply play and relax. The courtyard is now an
urban public space that invites participation.

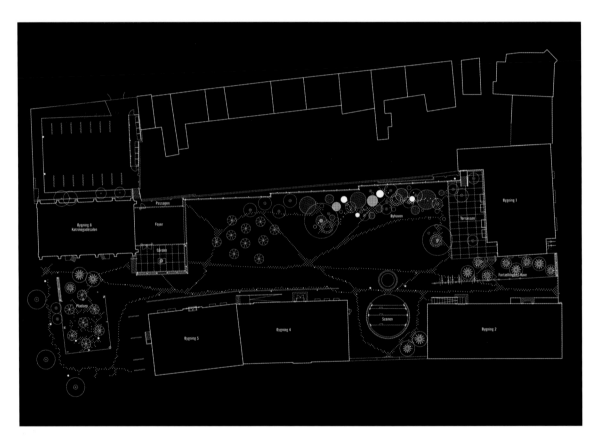

Site plan

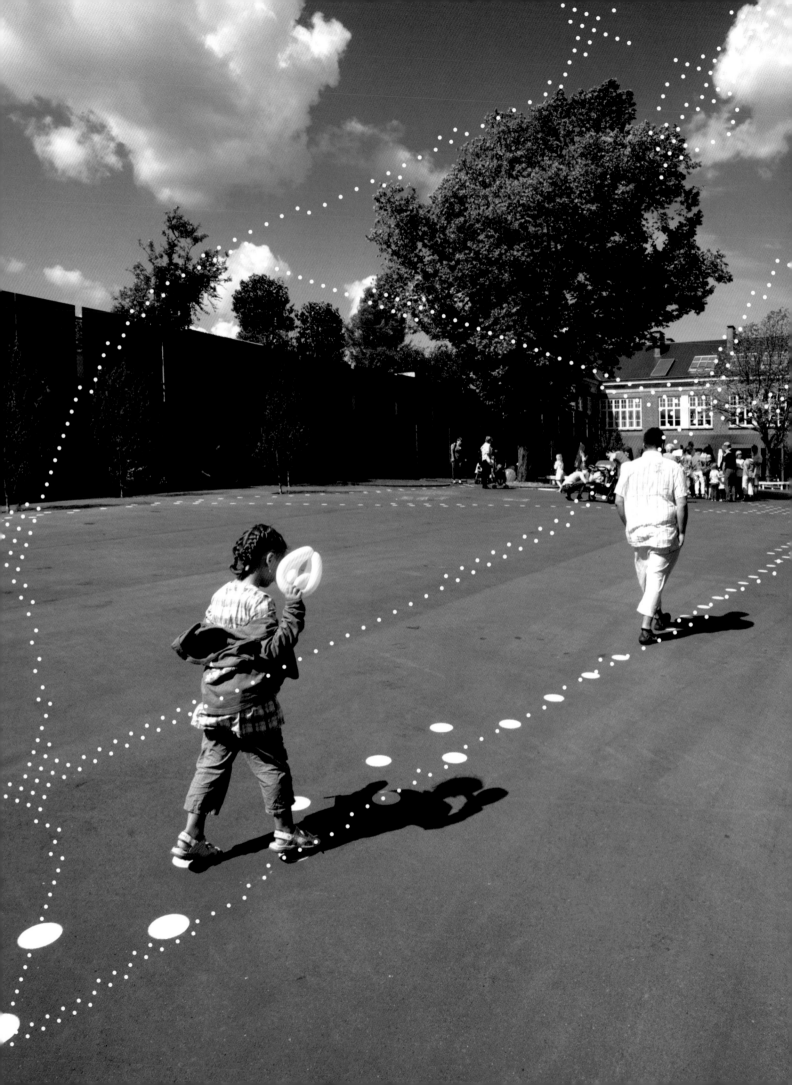

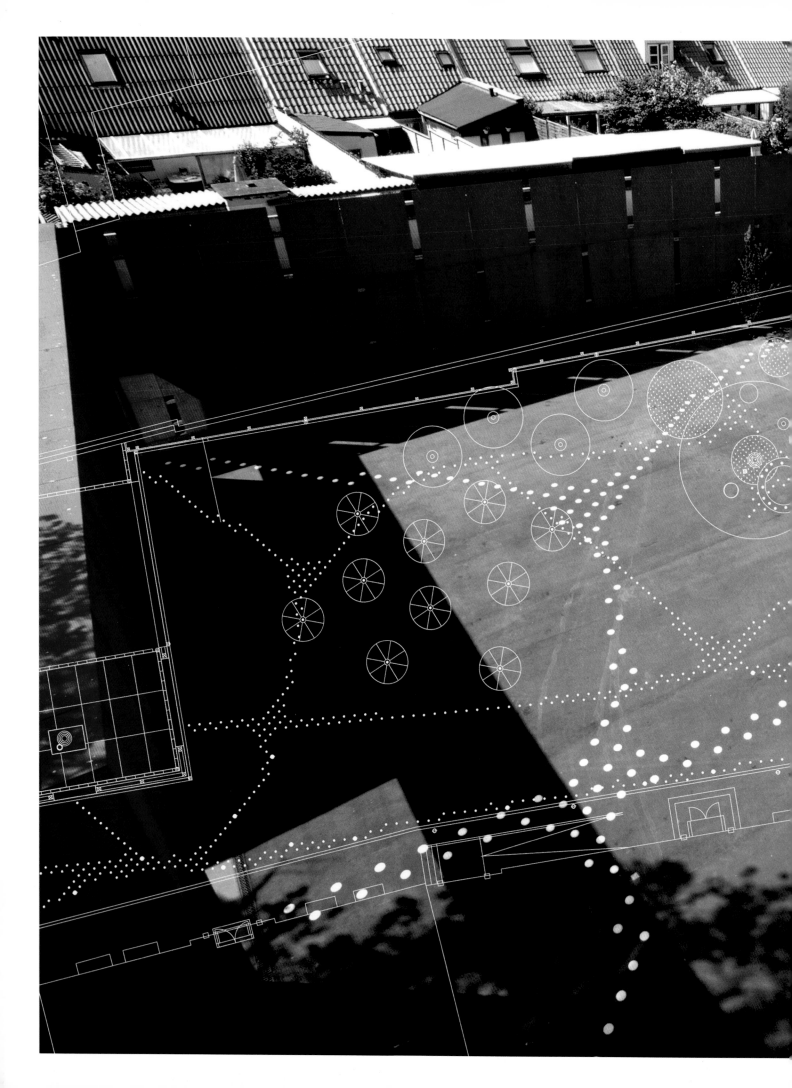

The schoolyard encompasses cultural and recreational activities such as an amphitheater, places for exhibitions and markets, and playgrounds and cafés with terraces for visitors to gather, sit, and relax in the sun.

# THE CITY DUNE / SEB BANK

Copenhagen, Denmark   2010

The Swedish SEB Bank recently had its Scandinavian headquarters built in a neighborhood near the harbor of Copenhagen as part of the process of that area's revitalization. SLA received the assignment to create an urban space that could integrate the new building with the existing surrounding area, the harbor, and the city of Copenhagen. The design team developed an area as a green and welcoming "open foyer" for the public and employees of the bank alike. The result is a sustainable and fully accessible urban space covering an area of 78,576 sq ft (7,300 m²) on top of an underground garage. Like a giant dune of sand or snow, the pavement slips in between and around the two buildings that constitute the bank institution, creating a feeling of wavy and upward movement. This "waviness" and the morphology of the terrain not only handles functional and technical demands from drainage, accessibility, and lighting to plantation, but also it offers a variety of routes for customers and employees of SEB, as well as ordinary Copenhageners, creating an ever changing urban space.

Acclimatization is an important aspect of the City Dune's design. Through the folding movements of the concrete, the surface reflects the sun's radiation, thereby creating a cooler microclimate during the hot months of the year.

**LANDSCAPE ARCHITECT**
SLA

**LOCATION**
Copenhagen, Denmark

**CLIENT**
SEB Bank & Pension

**COLLABORATORS**
Lundgaard & Tranberg Arkitekter (architect), Rambøll (structural engineer)

**AREA**
78,576 sq ft (7,300 m²)

**COST**
USD 6,168,960 (EUR 4,850,000)

**PHOTOGRAPHER**
SLA, Orev Vandingssystemer, Jens Lindhe

The City Dune, as the urban space quickly came to be called, is made of white concrete, borrowing its big, folding movement from the sand dunes of Northern Denmark and the snow mounds of the Scandinavian winter.

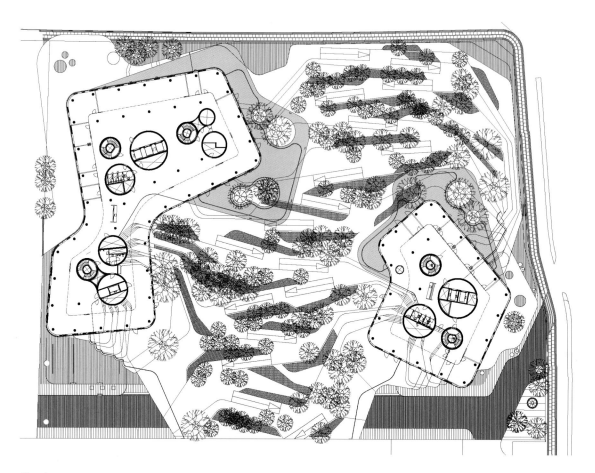

Site plan

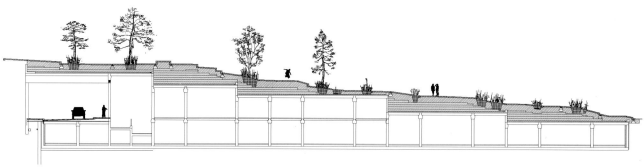

Section through parking garage

This seemingly lightweight structure blends seamlessly with the existing parkland. This academy is one of the world's greenest museums, having scored a total of 54 points in its LEED certification audit.

Lighting study representation

Partial section through site

# THE BROCKMAN HALL FOR PHYSICS

## Houston, TX, USA    2011

The Brockman Hall for Physics is a new facility at Rice University. The building and landscape provide a home for laboratories, classrooms, and offices and offer informal gathering spaces to foster conversation, debate, and the exchange of ideas.

The site lies between six existing buildings in the heart of what is known as the Courtyard of Science. The new facility is composed of two parallel long buildings running east-west. While the south building is anchored to the ground, the north one is elevated, connecting to the first through bridges and allowing the existing landscape to flow under it. To the south, the Brockman Hall is framed by the court-yard formed by the U-shaped George R. Brown building. The axis that bisects this courtyard continues through a sally port in the south building of Brockman Hall and terminates at the Hamman Hall building, which provides the new facility with a sense of enclosure. While the existing north-south axis is maintained, Brockman Hall establishes a new counter flow along the east-west axis that connects three formerly separate courts.

The crossing of the axis allows the space below the north building of Brockman Hall to become a central gathering place marked by a rectangular fountain.

**LANDSCAPE ARCHITECT**
The Office of James Burnett

**CLIENT**
Rice University

**COLLABORATORS**
KieranTimberlake (architect), Haynes Whaley Associates (Structural Consultant), CCRD Partners (MEP Consultant), Perkins + Will (Lab Consultant), Gilbane Construction Company (Construction Manager), Walter P Moore and Associates, Inc. (Civil Engineer), Arup Lighting (Lighting consultant), JEAcoustics (Acoustical Consultant), Ulrich Engineers, Inc. (Geotechnical Engineer), Jackson & Ryan Architects (Construction Administration / Consulting Architect)

**AREA**
The land area for the project: 145,000 sq ft (Areas C, D, H, F, G); the main site: 97,540 sq ft (Areas D, H); the GRB courtyard: 15,656 sq ft (Area G)

**COST**
USD 67 million

**PHOTOGRAPHER**
Hester + Hardaway Photography

Beyond the building site, the landscape responds
to the existing campus fabric and brings these
materials into the composition, allowing for
a seamless flow between old and new.

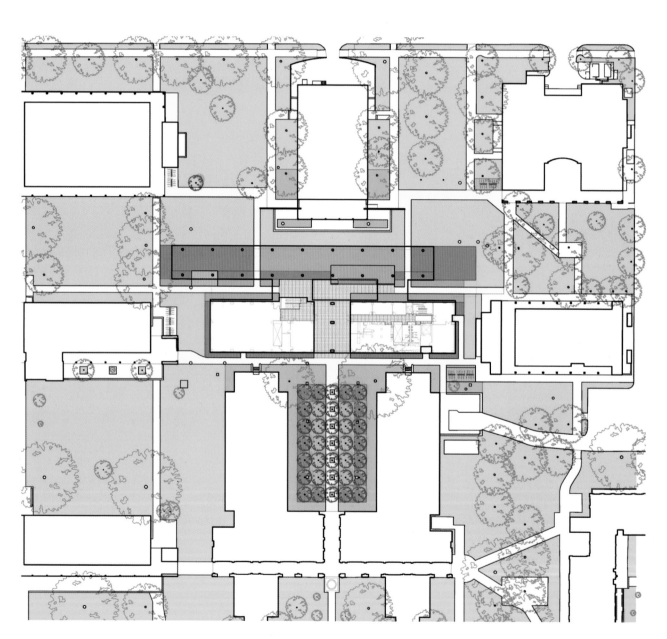

Site plan

e fountain provides both a cooling effect and
eflecting surface to allow natural light to play
 of the underside of the north building. It sits
 an Ipe deck, which is raised from the ground
provide a quiet space just off the path.

# IBM RIEKERPOLDER

## Amsterdam, the Netherlands    2005

The new IBM office building is part of the Riekerpolder Plaza urban development plan on the south side of Amsterdam. It includes a courtyard that is the heart of the building and a meeting point for the users of the facility. Water is extensively used as a design element, reflecting the wet nature of the surroundings.

The overall landscape design is composed of three main elements. In the first place, there are mirror ponds surrounding the building on the north, east, and west sides, which delimit the facility and reinforce its presence as a landmark in the urban fabric.

The second element is the green slope on the north, which acts as a base for the building while creating a natural barrier between the facility and the street.

And finally, there is the courtyard, in which flowing water in particular has been employed on a smaller scale. This courtyard is located at the bottom of a slope that descends in the direction of the main entrance to the office building on the east. A water ladder dissects the patio garden longitudinally, tracing the pedestrian path from level to level. Finally, it ends in a water spout at the entrance by way of a number of small ponds.

**LANDSCAPE ARCHITECTS**
Deltavormgroep

**CLIENT**
IBM

**COLLABORATORS**
William McDonough + Partners (Architecture and Community Design), Nelson Byrd Woltz (landscape architects)

**AREA**
n/a

**COST**
n/a

**PHOTOGRAPHER**
Deltavormgroep, Frank Colder, Picture 7

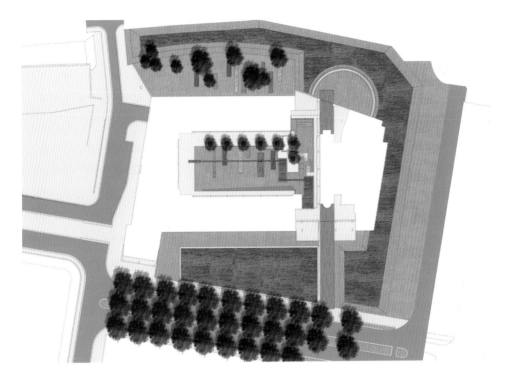

Site plan

Hand-drawn perspective view of the sloping site

The building's lobby and the courtyard levels are designed to be the meeting point of the various departments, promoting interoffice communication, casual meetings, and creative thinking.

e visual effect and sound of the falling and
owing water determine the nature of this place
nd offer a special atmosphere for pleasant
flection from the adjoining canteen.

# THE BROCHSTEIN PAVILION AT RICE UNIVERSITY

Houston, TX, USA   2008

The Rice University campus is distinguished by its neo-Byzantine architecture and formal long axes. In response to the need to create a new social hub in a special focus of the campus named Central Quadrangle, Thomas Phifer & Partners (architects) collaborated with the office of James Burnett, a landscape architect, creating an iconic landmark that would represent the intellectual crossroad of the campus. This collaboration resulted in a glass, steel, and aluminum pavilion that contrasts with the surrounding buildings. The pavilion sits on a concrete plaza that references the plan of the building. A concrete path, connecting the new structure with the 1940 library, bisects a grove of allee lacebark elms in a plane of decomposed granite. Two long, black concrete fountains filled with beach stones take center stage in the grove, filling the space with the murmur of running water. Other minor interventions, such as the creation of new concrete walks and the planting of specimen live oaks, respect the lightness and transparency of the pavilion, only to reinforce the spatial framework of the Quadrangle.

**LANDSCAPE ARCHITECT**
Office of James Burnett

**CLIENT**
Rice University

**COLLABORATORS**
Thomas Phifer & Partners (architect), Walter P Moore (civil engineering), Ulrich Engineers (geotechnical engineering), Altieri Sebor Wieber (MEP engineering), Haynes Whaley Associates (structural engineering), Construction Specifications (specifications), Fisher Marantz Stone (lighting design), Unbeck Group (contractor)

**AREA**
10,000 sq ft

**COST**
n/a

**AWARDS**
2010 Professional Awards from the American Society of Landscape Architects

**PHOTOGRAPHER**
The Office of James Burnett, Paul Hester

Rather than isolating the pavilion on a dramatic plinth,
the ground of the surrounding area was modeled
to harmonize the building with the landscape and
strengthen the existing framework of the campus.

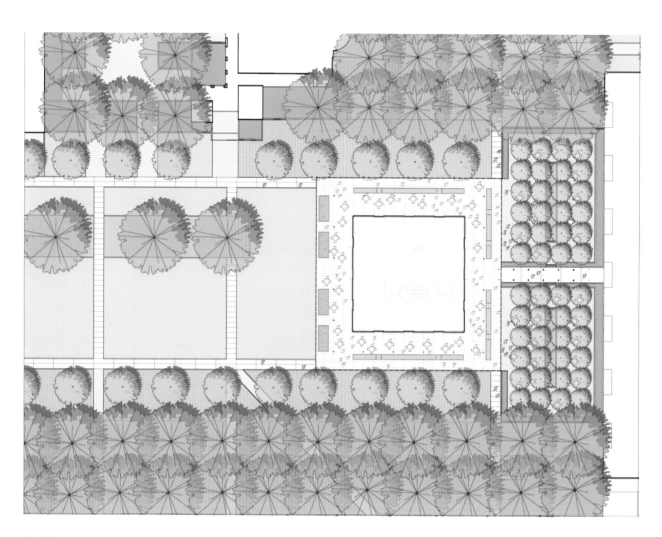

Site plan

# OUTDOOR LEARNING COURTYARD FOR THE
# NATURAL SCIENCES AT KEENE STATE COLLEGE

Keene, NH, USA    2007

The Keene State College Science Center Courtyard has provided the opportunity to redefine the landscape around the facilities constructed during World War II. The idea behind the project was to create a natural environment that motivates students to think in a broader context, making them more aware of their surroundings and their place in the community and in the natural world. In short, the courtyard is a place for education but also for relaxation and reflection. It provides a model outdoor field laboratory to promote botanical and horticultural awareness to both the college and the community. Also, it is intended to be a key link in the college's "Arboretum Walk," a self-guided tour through the central campus that highlights unique and mature plant specimens of historical and scientific value. Geology is the unifying component of the design, which incorporates geological layering, folding, faulting, erosion, and volcanism, while boulders from the surrounding region define character and scale. Decomposed granite along the building facades allows students and maintenance personnel access to plants. Botany faculty required the landscape architect to provide an evolutionary walk through New Hampshire plant groups.

**LANDSCAPE ARCHITECT**
Dirtworks Landscape Architecture

**LOCATION**
Keene, NH, USA

**CLIENT**
Keene State College

**AREA**
7,750 sq ft

**COST**
n/a

**AWARDS**
2007 Honor Award from the American Society of Landscape Architects—NY Chapter; 2008 Design Citation Award from the American Association of School Administrators (AASA); 2011 Honor Award in College and University Design from the Boston Chapter of the American Society of Landscape Architects (BSLA)

**PHOTOGRAPHER**
Andrew Bordwin, Mark Corliss, ESTO and Dirtworks, PC

The stone, selected in collaboration with the college's geology faculty, was chosen for suitability in conveying geological history. Specified and detailed for its beauty, durability, color, and texture, each stone contributes to the overall design of the paths.

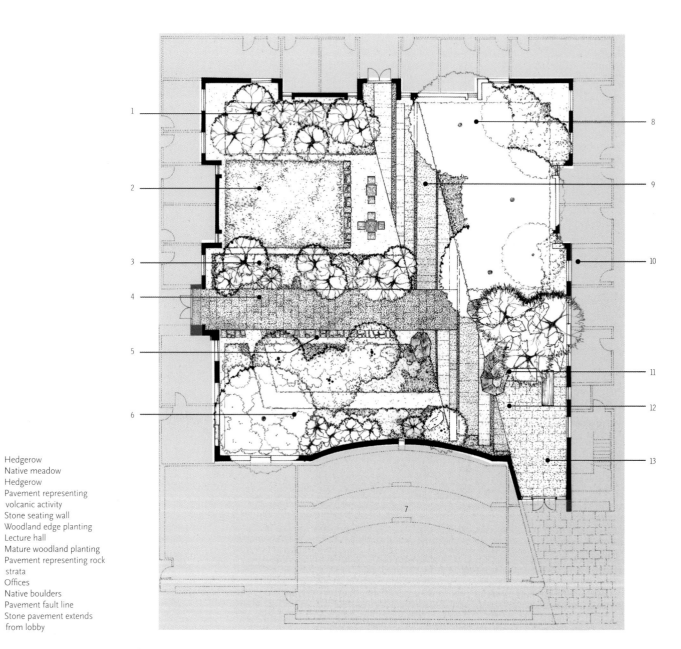

1.  Hedgerow
2.  Native meadow
3.  Hedgerow
4.  Pavement representing volcanic activity
5.  Stone seating wall
6.  Woodland edge planting
7.  Lecture hall
8.  Mature woodland planting
9.  Pavement representing rock strata
10. Offices
11. Native boulders
12. Pavement fault line
13. Stone pavement extends from lobby

Site plan

Plants from various communities represent
the systemic hierarchy of plant classification
and present an important demonstration of
seasonal change, plant growth, and maturity.

196

# THE ELIZABETH & NONA EVANS RESTORATIVE GARDEN AT THE CLEVELAND BOTANICAL GARDEN

## Cleveland, OH, USA    2006

The space designated for the new garden was small, sloped, and with a mature plant collection. It was adjacent to a busy dining terrace and provided the primary view from the the Cleveland Botanical Garden's gracious library. The program requirements were complex and construction was tied to an adjacent major building renovation and expansion project.

Because the garden was to be located within a public botanical garden where visitors are free to stroll, the need for privacy was an important consideration. The Cleveland Botanical Garden's board of directors, staff, and donors wanted a garden that was "beautiful, natural, lush, green; a setting that offers a range of opportunities, choices, and experiences; a setting engaging and enriching for all who visited." This mandate reflected the memory of a longtime friend and board member of the gardens and an early supporter of garden therapy who believed passionately that an "abundance of foliage, fragrances, blooms, and trees are invaluable elements of a healing garden environment." The resulting garden is a series of three unique settings, each with a distinct character and level of activity: one for quiet contemplation; one for both individual exploration and teaching large groups; and one for horticultural therapy.

**LANDSCAPE ARCHITECT**
Dirtworks Landscape Architecture

**LOCATION**
Cleveland, OH, USA

**CLIENT**
Cleveland Botanical Garden

**AREA**
12,000 sq ft

**COST**
n/a

**AWARDS**
2006 General Design Award of Honor from the American Society of Landscape Architects (ASLA)

**PHOTOGRAPHER**
K. Duteil

The Restorative Garden has the mission to "blend education, social responsibility, cultural and environmental stewardship" helping "people of all ages, backgrounds, and abilities appreciate and benefit from the positive role that plants play in their lives."

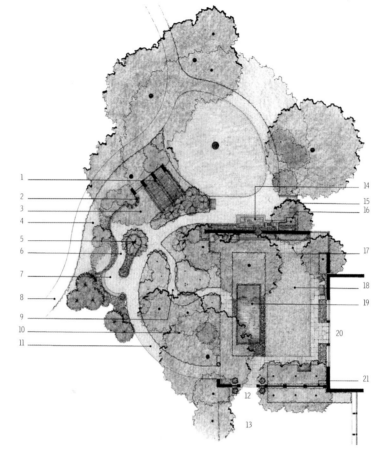

A GARDEN FOR
HORTICULTURAL
THERAPY

1. Trellis and storage
2. Stepped planters
3. Group activities
4. Perennial embankment
5. Raised planters for therapy and display
6. Sensory walk
7. Welcome area
8. Public walk
9. "Secret path"
10. "Hidden" garden
11. Main path
12. Entry
13. Terrace

A GARDEN FOR LEARNING
AND EXPLORING

14. Demonstration wall with featured plantings, water elements and stone
15. Overlook with braille rail
16. Shade garden

A GARDEN FOR
CONTEMPLATION

17. Overlook with Braille rail
18. Lawn panel
19. Reflecting pool
20. Library
21. Stone wall

Site plan

1. Public walk
2. Perennial embankment
3. Sensory walk
4. Raised planters for therapy and display
5. Main path
6. "Hidden" garden

Section through therapy garden

1. Contemplative garden above
2. Shade garden
3. Water features / Water garden
4. Stepped planters and garden niches integral to wall for therapy and display

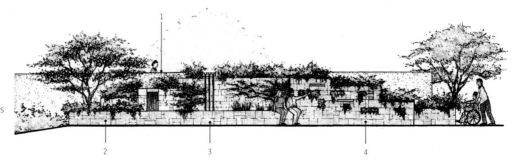

Elevation of demonstration wall

# CONTIWEG SECONDARY SCHOOL

## Vienna, Austria   2010

Contiweg Secondary School is organized along an axis that connects the forecourt with the interior courtyard and sport grounds of the school at the back. The central part of the project is the courtyard, dominated by a stage and a tribune. It presents a higher level of complexity, which echoes the architecture that surrounds it. For instance, the lentil shapes are a decorative leitmotif that can be found as openings in the main facade of the building and on the ground as flower beds. They give the school its special profile and provide for an unmistakable identity. A distinct experience is provided to students through specially designed furniture, amenities, and utilities such as a "bicycle bench." Within this framework, several design ideas for the open space are adapted to fit the school's own interests and offer the possibility to grow. To provide the open space with structure, learning pathways with trees were created. As in an arboretum, where one can find a wide variety of species, students are able to discover and study local trees in the forecourt and exotic species in the school's garden.

**LANDSCAPE ARCHITECT**
idealice

**CLIENT**
Bundesimmobiliengesellschaft (BIG)

**COLLABORATORS**
Atelier Heiss

**AREA**
n/a

**COST**
n/a

**PHOTOGRAPHER**
idealice

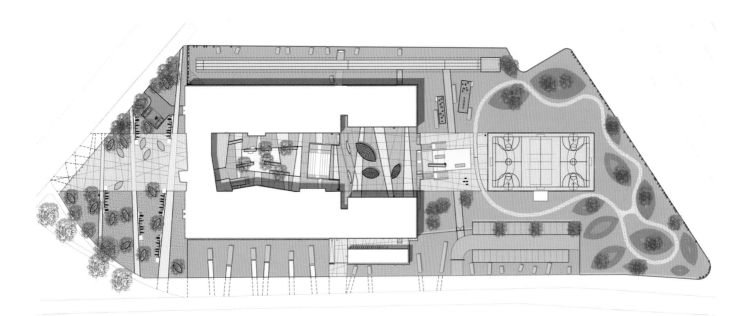

Site plan

A sports field and two running tracks are integrated into the design of the school gardens. Blossoming bushes alongside the tracks demonstrate what colorful grounds one can expect to find within the school complex.

# ARBORETUM AT HOSPITAL KLAGENFURT

## Klagenfurt, Austria 2010

As part of a plan to connect the new construction with the former hospital and provide the complex with formal unity, the arboretum consists of nineteen courtyards that imbue the facility with greenery. Starting at the Glan River in the north, the landscape flows into the hospital, becoming increasingly artificial. Various tree species found on the banks of the Glan River were selected as a design template for each of the six patio units. Hence there are oak, cherry, maple, and willow patios in the Surgical-Medical Center (CMZ), and lime and wild fruit patios in the Supply and Disposal Center (VEZ). The two centers are connected by an alley of ginkgos.

The northern courtyards of the CMZ is planted with wild species of oak, cherry, maple, willow trees, and lawn. In contrast, the southern courtyards are defined by sparse specimen trees and decorative gravel and colored glass in steel planters that make for a more abstract landscape. In the VEZ 's linden tree courtyards, yellow perennials and blossoms shape the space. The red wild fruit courtyards are equipped with gabions with built-in seats to create a meeting place and recreation area.

**LANDSCAPE ARCHITECT**
idealice landschaftsarchitektur

**CLIENT**
KABEG Management

**COLLABORATORS**
Feichtinger Architectes; Priebernig.
Architekten + Ingenieure; Architects
Collective; Müller&Klinger; FCP Fritsch,
Chiari & Partner

**AREA**
645,834 sq ft (60,000 m²)

**COST**
Aprox. USD 2.92 million
(EUR 2.3 million)

**PHOTOGRAPHER**
idealice

The texture of the bark of each species of tree was a source of inspiration for the arrangement and shape of the terraces and planting beds, while the coloring of the leaf and blooms determined the color of the planters and of the ground treatment.

Site plan

216

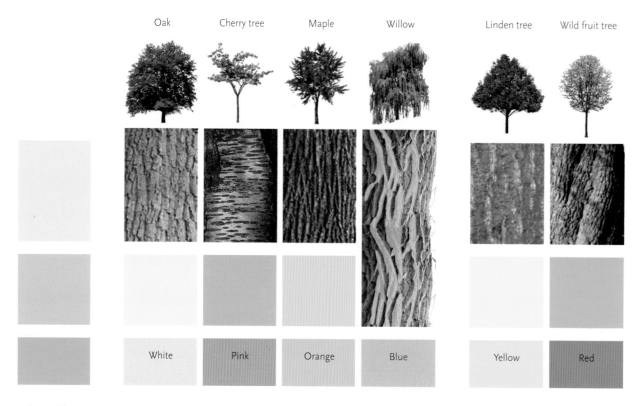

Oak  Cherry tree  Maple  Willow  Linden tree  Wild fruit tree

White  Pink  Orange  Blue  Yellow  Red

Color and form conceptual diagram

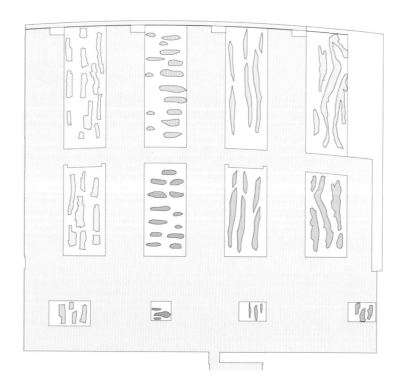
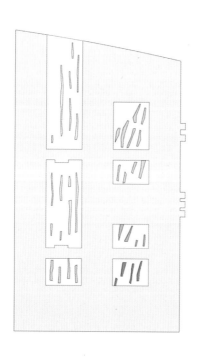

Diagrammatic plan of the patios

# UNIVERSITY OF MINNESOTA DULUTH, LABORATORY SCIENCE BUILDING

## Minneapolis, MN, USA   2007

The site plan for the new Laboratory Science Building (LSB) is based on the concept of "Science on Display." The architect and landscape designer have worked together to generate coherent relationships between interior and exterior and elements of transparency to allow for activities normally conducted in opacity. This collaboration resulted in two outdoor courtyards designed as a transitional space for pedestrian circulation and as a gathering space for students, faculty, and staff. The upper courtyard, located in the northwest elbow of the building, is intended to serve as a gathering area, as well as a contemplative space. It is bordered by a grove of deciduous trees and a seat wall, and is embellished with three sculptural cubes made of perforated metal and lit from within. The lower courtyard is located to the south of the LSB and features a two-tiered experimental garden pool separated by a curved concrete weir. New groves of northern forest trees complement the two courtyard designs. These trees help tie the building and its outdoor spaces to the campus landscape and to the overarching native ecosystem of northern Minnesota, quietly reinforcing the idea that UMD is a uniquely Northern Minnesota university.

**LANDSCAPE ARCHITECT**
Oslund and Assoc.

**LOCATION**
Minneapolis, MN, USA

**CLIENT**
University of Minnesota Duluth

**COLLABORATORS**
Stanius Johnson Architects, Inc. (Architect of record for the building), Ross Barney + Jankowski, Inc. (Design Architect for the building), Meyer, Borgman and Johnson, Inc. (Structural Engineer), MSA Professional Services (Civil Engineer), Affiliated Engineers (Mechanical & Electrical Engineers), Max Gray Construction, Inc. (General Contractor for the site work), M.A. Mortenson (General Contractor for the building), Oscar J. Boldt Construction Co. (Cost Consultant).

**AREA**
1 acre

**COST**
n/a

**AWARDS**
2007 Design Honor Award presented by the American Society of Landscape Architects; 2007 Design Award of Excellence presented by the American Society of Landscape Architects, Minnesota Chapter; 2005 Design Merit Award for Unbuilt Works presented by the American Society of Landscape Architects, Minnesota Chapter

**PHOTOGRAPHER**
Oslund and Assoc.

Artist's impression

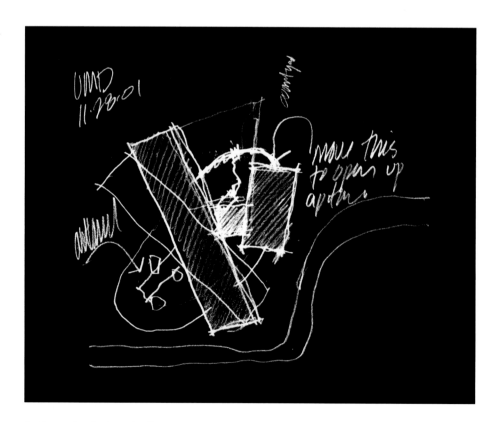

Architectural preliminary sketch

e pool functions as a destination for storm water off from the surrounding site and the roof of LSB. The upper pool is a water garden, with a ecial emphasis on the cultivation of wild rice.

The garden will be used as an outdoor laboratory for
science students and faculty. The building incorporates
an atrium and glass-walled classrooms, as well as
interactive outdoor learning and contemplative spaces.

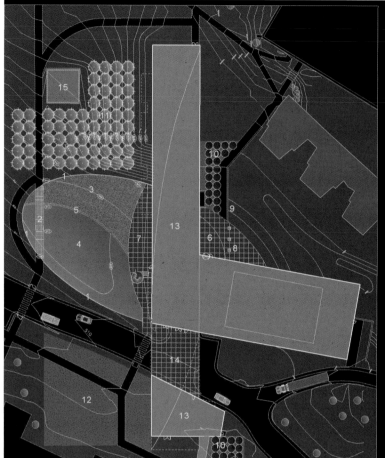

1. Corten wall
2. Metal bridge
3. Upper pool with wild rice
4. Lower pool
5. Concrete weir
6. Upper courtyard
7. Lower courtyard
8. Metal cubes
9. Seat wall
10. Deciduous tree grove
11. Coniferous tree grove
12. Dogwood planting
13. Laboratory Science Building
14. Building link above road
15. Cooling tower

Site plan

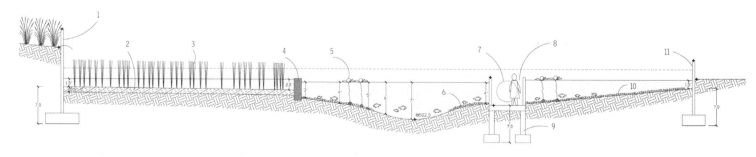

Pond section (study diagram)

1. Corten retaining wall
2. Wild rice sediment
3. Wild rice
4. Concrete or wood edge
5. Lily pads
6. Sandy gravel
7. Fish window at the
   end of ramp
8. Viewing ramp
9. Concrete or steel pillar
10. Sandy gravel
11. Corten wall

# THE NEW AUSTRALIAN GARDENS AT THE NGA CANBERRA

## Canberra ACT, Australia    2010

The National Gallery of Australia and its surrounding sculpture garden, designed respectively by Edwards Madigan Torzillo and Briggs, and Harry Howard and Associates were completed in 1982. In 2005, in conjunction with significant works that consisted in the expansion of the gallery and the creation of the Australian Garden, the project also included a Skyspace sculpture titled *Within Without* by U.S. artist James Turrell.

PTW Architects were commissioned to extend the building and McGregor Coxall landscape architects were given the role of remaking the public realm and designing the new Australian Garden. Located on the existing parking lot, the main garden was designed around retained eucalyptus trees. Two planar lawns, designed to host events such as temporary art exhibitions and garden parties, form the main space. Sustainable design principles include the choice of low-embodied energy materials and the harvest of storm water for internal reuse and for irrigation of the new garden. Extensive indigenous planting was used to form a dense frame of bush land around the geometrical design. Australian slate and granite, concrete aggregates, and gravel sourced in local quarries were used to be consistent with the material palette of the existing works.

**LANDSCAPE ARCHITECT**
McGregor Coxall

**LOCATION**
Canberra ACT, Australia

**CLIENT**
National Gallery of Australia

**COLLABORATORS**
PTW Architects (architects), Cardno Young (civil), Birzulis Associates (structural), Steensen Varming (mechanical), George Sexton (lighting), Manteena (construction management), Urban Contractors (contractor)

**AREA**
8.9 acres (3.6 ha)

**COST**
n/a

**PHOTOGRAPHER**
Christian Borchert, John Gollings, Simon Grimmett

McGregor Coxall ensured the new landscape embraced the geometric design principles of the Madigan design to proportion new elements. Extending the triangular grid of the original building created a framework for the location and arrangement of significant new features.

Schematic design—master plan

The centerpiece of the garden is a pond into which the prominent sculpture *Within Without* appears to be sunken. In the center of the skyspace is a basalt stupa. Visitors move through the stupa to the carefully lit oculus, which opens to the sky above.

# THE NEW YORK TIMES BUILDING
# LOBBY GARDEN

New York, NY, USA   2007

The New York Times building lobby emerges as an iconic courtyard in one of New York City's densest neighborhoods. Its minimalist design emphasizes a poetic approach that references the Hudson River Valley woodland landscape and creates a strong natural statement, harmonizing the building's design elements.

As part of Renzo Piano Building Workshop and FX Fowle Architect's design team, HM White led the courtyard design—considered the heart and soul of The New York Times building. As a counterpoint to its bustling Times Square neighborhood, the open courtyard's location reveals a serene, secluded spot at the heart of this man-made construct. The garden court evolved into a birch grove, and a mixture of shade-loving sedge grasses and native ferns. The ground cover species were selected for their ability to establish a uniform green mantle and to perform consistently within a wide range of light and moisture conditions. The "hillocks" provide sculptural form and draw attention to the solitary timber walk that bridges over its sensitive landscape as the only means of access. The design emphasizes a bold simplicity to create a strong natural statement that harmonizes rather than competes with the building's design elements.

**ARCHITECTS**
HM White Site Architects in collaboration with Cornelia Oberlander Architects

**CLIENT**
The New York Times Company

**COLLABORATORS**
Renzo Piano Building Workshop and FXFowle Architects (building architects), Thornton Tomasetti (engineer), Ekistics Planning & Design (microclimatic), Office for visual Interaction (lighting), Treewise Organics (arborist / soil food web specialist), High Ridge Farms Nursery (nurseries), Kelco Construction (landscape contractor), Amec Construction (general contractor)

**AREA**
3,500 sq ft

**COST**
n/a

**AWARDS**
2008 Architecture Honor Award from the American Institute of Architects (AIA) New York Chapter; 2010 Honor Award from the American Society of Landscape Architects (ASLA); 2006 Research and Communication Merit Award

**PHOTOGRAPHER**
Aaron Booher, Huei Ming Juang

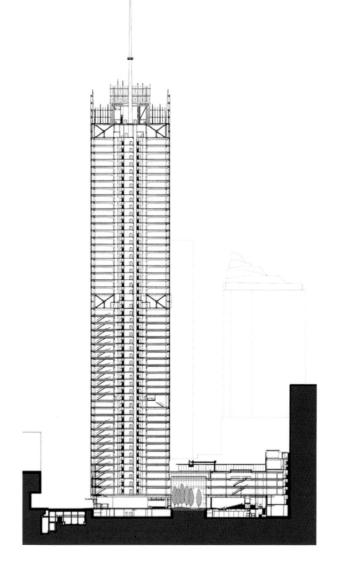

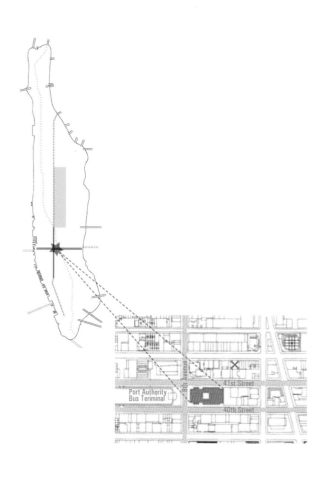

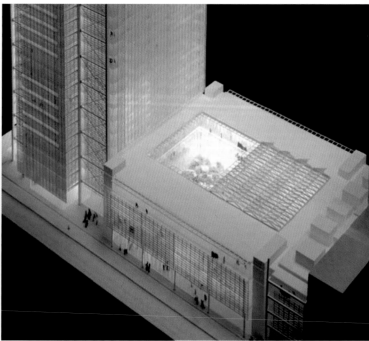

Model views, site context, and building section

asonal solar radiation and wind levels
re mapped at strategic times of the year
reveal the environmental variations, while
owing conditions were analyzed to determine
ecies selection and arrangements were
de to ensure long-term sustainability.

The iconic courtyard is an identifying design element of the New York Times Company's headquarters. It benefits from the face of the building's architectural transparency and its central position for surrounding public and office spaces.

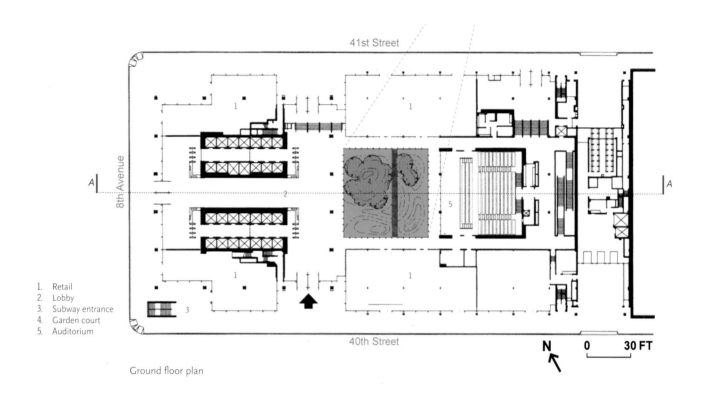

1. Retail
2. Lobby
3. Subway entrance
4. Garden court
5. Auditorium

Ground floor plan

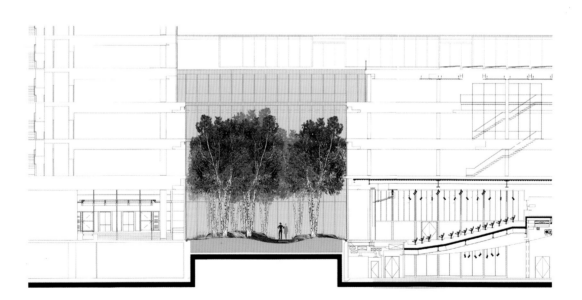

Section through lobby, garden courtyard, and auditorium

The glass and steel building showcases a 70-foot square open-air woodland garden situated directly on Manhattan schist bedrock, the site's only un-excavated area. The building's transparent quality enable nature to be revealed at the building's core.

# BEATFUSE

## New York, NY, USA   2006

"BEATFUSE!" was created on the occasion of an annual summer event at New York City's MOMA P.S.1—theYoung Architects Program Warm Up. It is a structure made to be experienced from within rather than from outside. The large triangular outdoor space is partially covered with seven shells manufactured and assembled in a workshop and later deployed on-site. Forming an irregular grid, these shells are curved and able to span the 20 to 30 feet required. The shells are then covered with a skin of polypropylene scales approximately 2'-6" × 2'-6" in size and attached only at one point to the structure. This allows wind and rain to move through them without excessively taxing the structure with lateral or lifting loads while providing soft shade.

Just as the shells contract and expand to facilitate installation, and the scales gently open to let wind through, the pools can grow to their maximum footprint or shrink into discrete circular ponds. This allows the inclusion of larger crowds and access to slightly raised levels where one can stand, sit, or dance. The sandbox gallery is designated as the Caldarium. It has little to no shade and features an array of radial chaise lounges for sunbathing, as well as a large soaking pool.

**ARCHITECT**
OBRA Architects

**LOCATION**
New York, NY, USA

**CLIENT**
The Museum of Modern Art and P.S.1 Contemporary Art Center

**COLLABORATORS**
Robert Silman Associates (structural design); Nat Oppenheimer, Transsolar Energietechnik GmbH (climate engineering); David White, Tillett Lighting Design (lighting design); Linnaea Tillett, Stephen Horner, Yeune Kyue Kim, Dr. Gerald Palevsky PE (pool design); Omnivore (graphic design); Alice Chung, Karen Hsu, Site Assembly, (concertina mockup & video); Terry Chance, Kevin Karpinski, Panagiotis Chatzitsakyris, BEATFUSE

**COMPLETION DATE**
2006

**AREA**
n/a

**COST**
USD 70,000

**PHOTOGRAPHER**
OBRA Architects

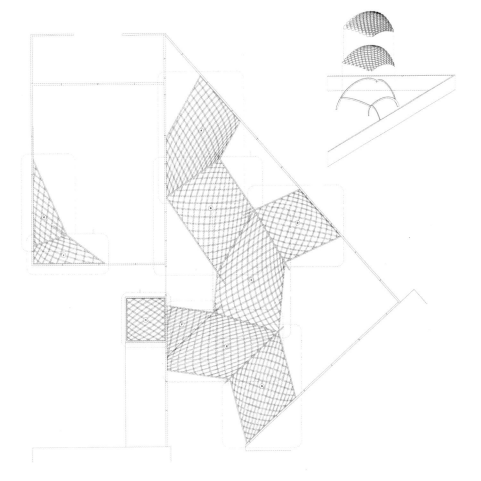

Roof plan

Floor plan

Water misters are provided throughout the project.
They are protected under three-foot diameter
steel mesh hemispheres that also contain a light
fixture. The light and mist combination produces
an effect of constantly changing shapes.

246

Water mister plan, elevation and sections

# PUBLIC SPACES
# AROUND
# RESIDENTIAL
# DEVELOPMENTS

# COOPERATIVE HOUSING KATZENBACH

## Zurich, Switzerland    2010

The new housing for Katzenbach is part of a general transformation process on the edge of Zurich, replacing older garden developments with high-density housing. The "Tree Courtyards" continue the larger scale of the surrounding woods set forth with the play of light and shadow among high deciduous trees on an open ground plane. However, the "Flowering Courtyards" lie above underground parking, where only smaller vegetation is possible. These gardens interpret anew the private gardens in the former row house typology with a dense fill of vegetative colors, forms, and textures.

The central plaza, a playing and meeting space with a garden pavilion, follows the logic of the "Tree Courtyards." Within the rigid placement of the housing buildings, a soft, ephemeral atmosphere is created using the play of light and shadow made by the tree canopies overhead. The light roof of leaves, the vertical trunks, and the shadows cast upon the ground are the determining elements of the design, echoed in variations within the design. A wide variety of uses for diverse user groups are woven inconspicuously into the plaza, such as the climbing landscape, sand and water, play elements, grill space, swings, and enormous seating elements.

**LANDSCAPE ARCHITECT**
Robin Winogrond Landscape Architect

**LOCATION**
Zurich, Switzerland

**CLIENT**
Baugenossenschaft Glattal Zürich

**COLLABORATORS**
Zita Cotti Architekten

**AREA**
123,785 sq ft (11,500 m²)

**COST**
USD 100 million (CHF 91 million)

**PHOTOGRAPHER**
Robin Winogrond Landscape Architect

The ground plane of the plaza emulates the projection of light and shadow through the trees and encourages users to meander through the space. A water plane—level with the paving—reflects the open sky or leafy roof depending on the location of the viewer.

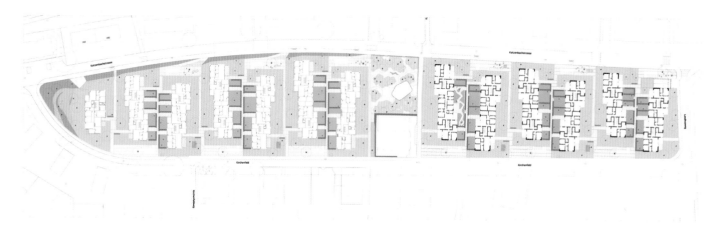

Site plan

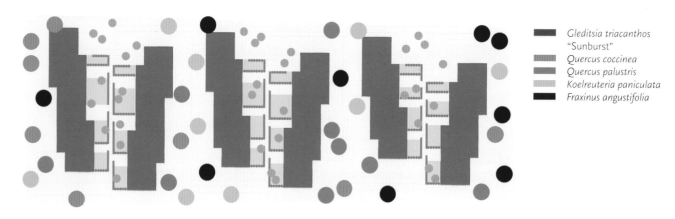

*Gleditsia triacanthos* "Sunburst"
*Quercus coccinea*
*Quercus palustris*
*Koelreuteria paniculata*
*Fraxinus angustifolia*

Diagram of the vegetation color pattern in the fall

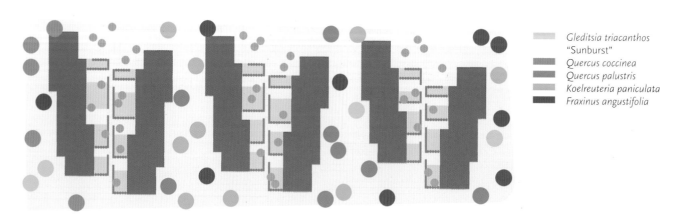

*Gleditsia triacanthos* "Sunburst"
*Quercus coccinea*
*Quercus palustris*
*Koelreuteria paniculata*
*Fraxinus angustifolia*

Diagram of the vegetation color pattern in the summer

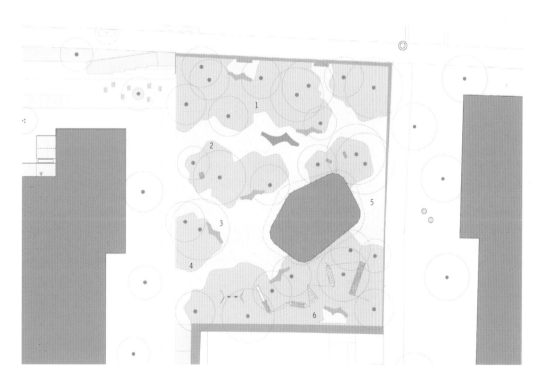

1. Bocce ball
2. Surface of water
3. Grill space
4. Sand and water
5. Entrance pavilion
6. Climbing landscape

Programmatic plan of the Central Plaza

Seating elements dissolve themselves into the language of the voids between leaves. The tree trunks are echoed in the dark columns of the pavilion and the play landscape made up of cables and posts winding between trees.

# EUSEBIO BARQUÍN MIJARES PARK

Santa Cruz de Bezana, Spain    2008

The park is confined between two buildings, each forming a wide angle. The resulting space is a trapezoid with accesses at both ends of one of its diagonals. This park, designed as segments of vegetation, provides access to homes, offices, and commercial spaces, becoming a public park for the community.

Each segment of vegetation has its own identity, resulting in small gardens and tree groves where the contrast between the different plant textures, colors, and terrain morphologies plays a key role to produce sensations in those who visit them.

The trails make their way through the planted areas, which in certain places seem to narrow the granite, concrete, and slate paths, creating the illusion of walking through a dark forest and its undergrowth. This idea is reinforced by the play of light and shadow produced by the foliage.

The park was created with the idea in mind to bring nature into the lives of the people who walk through the park on a daily basis. The chromatic changes in the vegetation according to the different seasons intensifies visitors' experiences, stimulating all the senses.

**DESIGNERS**
David Añíbarro and Javier de Diego

**CLIENT**
Planvica (developer and builder)

**COLLABORATORS**
Fabio Organai, Irrigation Systems
F. Santamaría

**AREA**
46,974 sq ft (4,364 m²)

**COST**
USD 9,7968 per sq ft (EUR 77,51 per m²)

**PHOTOGRAPHER**
David Añíbarro

om north to south and from east to west, the
ved paths are the backbone of the park. They
nerate interpretations of natural spaces and
rdens with different vegetation species. Trees,
rubs, and plants, along with the modeling of
e terrain, divide these natural spaces, creating
nes with different levels of seclusion.

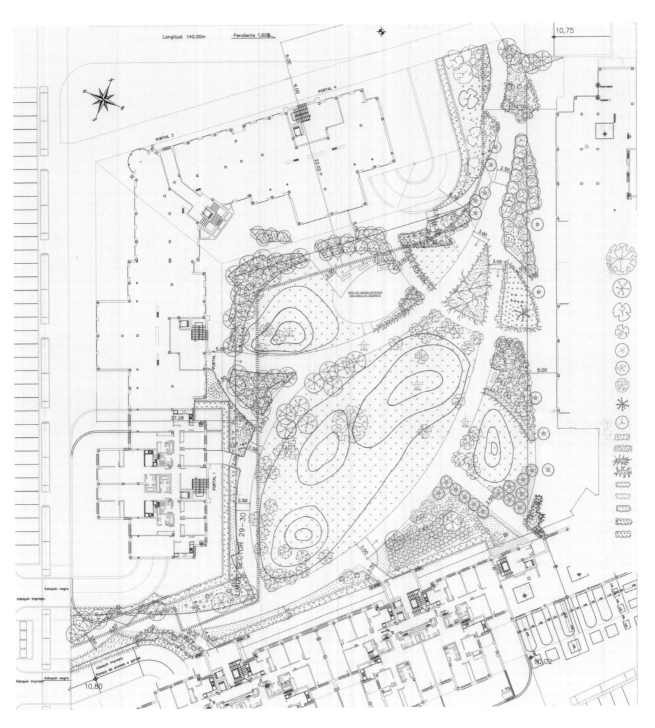

Site plan

# BAAN SANSUK

## Nongkae, Hua Hin, Prachuapkhirikhan, Thailand    2010

Baan Sansuk is an exclusive residential development located in Thailand's popular beach resort of Hua Hin. However, with its long and narrow layout perpendicular to the beach, most apartments don't have views of the ocean. The landscape design is developed around the idea of bringing the views to the complex, formed by two rows of buildings facing each other. They are separated by a 230-meter-long strip with planted areas and pools that connect the main lobby with the beach. These pools fulfill different functions for the enjoyment of the residents: A pool for children to play in is near the lobby, and sinuously shaped reflecting pools are part of a Zen-like garden design of lawns and trees, boulders, and boat-like planters. The "cascading pool" is an area for lounging, with large comfortable chairs. Closer to the beach, at the mouth of the U-shaped development, is the "Ocean Pool." These water features are delimited by paths, bridges, and wood decks, with chairs creating a dynamic composition that residents can interact with and also enjoy from their apartments up above.

**LANDSCAPE ARCHITECT**
TROP (TROP: terrains + open space)

**CLIENT**
Sansiri

**COLLABORATORS**
Dhevanand Architects

**AREA**
125,000 sq ft (11,613 m²)

**COST**
n/a

**PHOTOGRAPHER**
Pattarapol Jormkhanngen, Pok Kobkongsanti

Site plan

a Hin, which means "stone head" in Thai,
akes reference to the boulders found on
e famous beach. The design, inspired by
s natural setting, features various boulders
bring the beach experience into view.

# ORNAMENTAL POND

## Heemstede, the Netherlands    2008

HOSPER developed a design for the land of the Hageveld estate that included an ornamental pond on top of an underground garage. The estate had previously been a seminary, and part of it had been occupied by a secondary school. While the architectural structures of Hageveld still kept their allure, the vegetation had been neglected and the front of the building was vacant. In 2002, the new owner wished to transform this vacant section into a block of sixty luxury apartments. This development required the construction of a parking garage. So as not to alter the original grounds of the estate, it was decided to build the parking structure underground in front of the building. The original plan of the estate is based on three concentric shells: The building forms the central core; it is surrounded by a formal garden; which, in turn, is surrounded by farmland. The two outer shells function as a park. The design consisted of the improvement of the park vegetation and its water system and the restoration and expansion of the paths. The quality of this representative side of the estate has been retained and enhanced by the construction of a large, new ornamental pond that is "invisibly" bisected by the entrance to the underground car park.

**LANDSCAPE ARCHITECT**
HOSPER landscape architects

**CLIENT**
Hopman Interheem Group

**COLLABORATORS**
MYJ groep architects, Stijlgroep, Braaksma & Roos architects, Hermine van der Does (artist)

**AREA**
7,858 sq ft (730 m²)

**COST**
n/a

**PHOTOGRAPHER**
Pieter Kers

Delimited by a Corten steel rim, the ornamental pond has light shafts that allow daylight into the underground garage. At night, the openings covered with colored glass panels filter the light from the garage to create a very special visual effect.

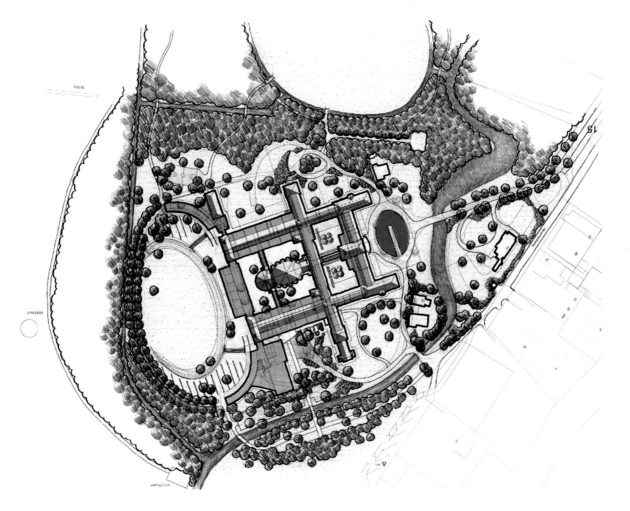

Site plan

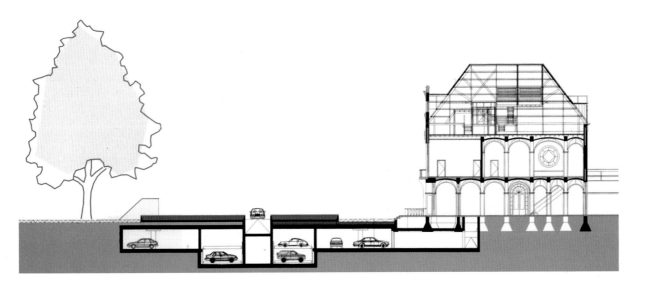

Section

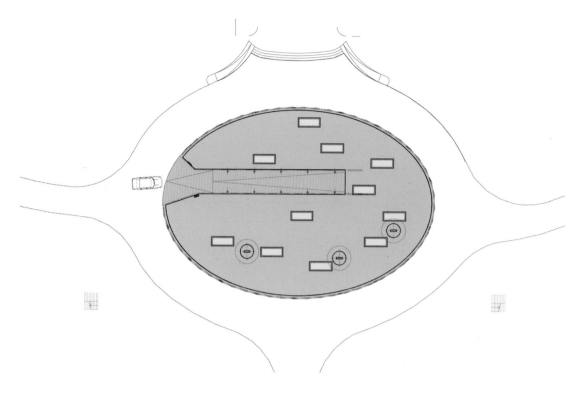

Pond detail plan

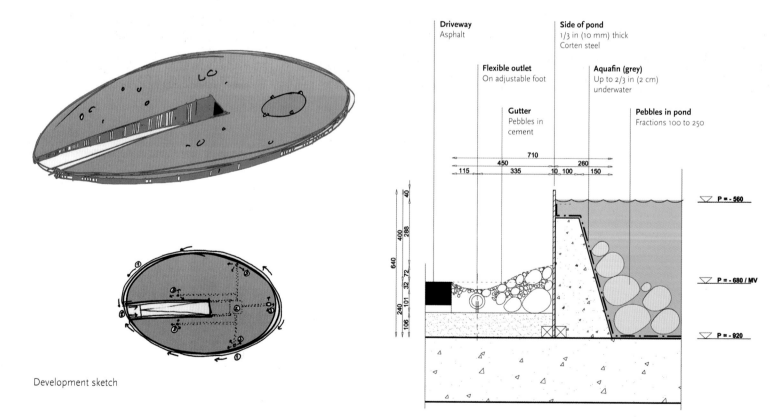

Development sketch

Pond edge details

**Driveway**
Asphalt

**Side of pond**
1/3 in (10 mm) thick
Corten steel

**Flexible outlet**
On adjustable foot

**Aquafin (grey)**
Up to 2/3 in (2 cm)
underwater

**Gutter**
Pebbles in
cement

**Pebbles in pond**
Fractions 100 to 250

710
450
115    335    10  100   260   150

40
400
288
640
32 72
240
106 101

▽ P = - 560

▽ P = - 680 / MV

▽ P = - 920

# PLAYGROUNDS, ZOOS, BOTANICAL GARDENS, AND CEMETERIES

# SCULPTURAL PLAYGROUND, SCHULBERG

## Wiesbaden, Germany   2011

An elevated land overlooking the city center of Wiesbaden created an opportunity for an outstanding public space attracting people of all ages and ethnic backgrounds. The site is dominated by a large sculptural structure that serves as a playground.

It is defined by three main elements. The first is a spatial sculpture consisting of two green steel pipes winding and floating between trees. In between this structure, a tensed climbing net creates a continuous surface. In plan view, the pentagonal shape of the structure is inspired by the historic shape of the city of Wiesbaden, while the side views make reference to urban situations and generatie vista points. The second element of the playground is constituted by an artificial topography within the limits of the climbing sculpture. Small mounds made of green soft rubber granulate rise from a bed of sand and offer playing opportunities for small kids. Finally, the third element is a wide pathway around the playground with benches for parents and the elderly, who come to watch their children play or to enjoy the views over Wiesbaden. To complete the design, an elegantly rounded curb made from anthracite follows the pentagonal shape of the playground and separates it from the boulevard.

**LANDSCAPE ARCHITECTS**
ANNABAU Architecture and Landscape

**CLIENT**
City of Wiesbaden

**COLLABORATORS**
Niehues Winkler Ingenieure
(engineering)

**AREA**
34,982 sq ft (3,250 m²)

**COST**
n/a

**PHOTOGRAPHER**
Hans Joosten

Together with a nearby reconstructed museum, the monument of the former synagogue, and a restored Roman aqueduct from the third century, Schulberg is the catalyst that transformed this previously neglected area.

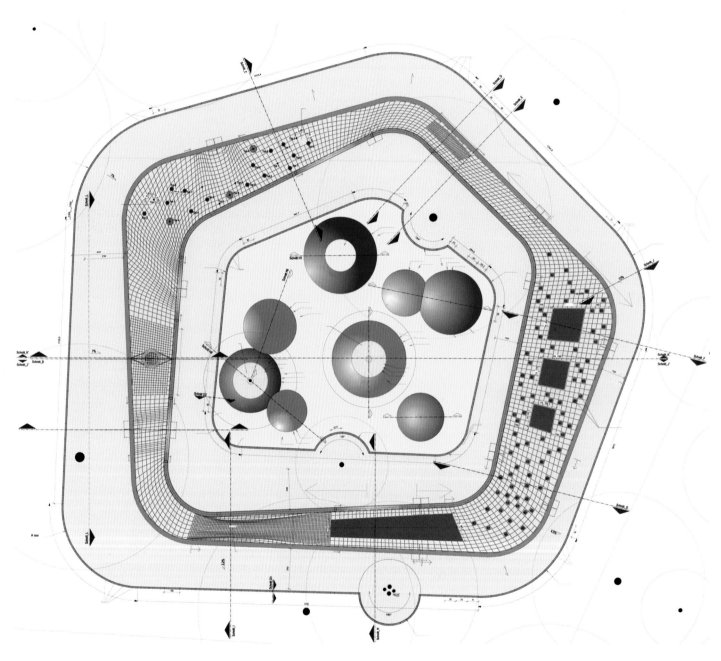

Site plan

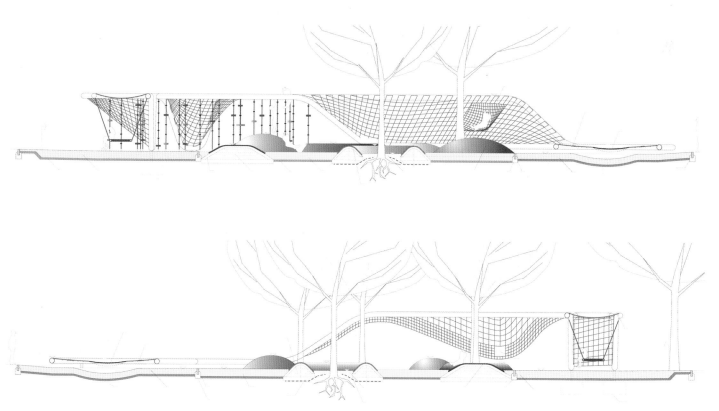

Sections

Various stopovers in the climbing structure are bouncing membranes, a tunnel, a swing, and a slide. The bright, attractive green color of the sculpture corresponds with the trees on-site and the adjacent reddish brick buildings.

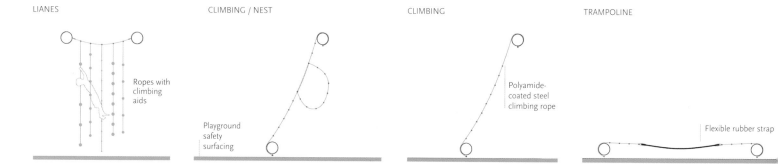

LIANES       CLIMBING / NEST       CLIMBING       TRAMPOLINE

Ropes with climbing aids

Playground safety surfacing

Polyamide-coated steel climbing rope

Flexible rubber strap

Actions diagram

SLIDE

TUNNEL

TIRE SWING

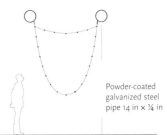

Powder-coated
galvanized steel
pipe 14 in × ¼ in

# BAHNDECKEL THERESIENHÖHE

## Munich, Germany    2010

A concrete slab over underground train tracks offers the opportunity to create a new open space between Bavaria Park, West Park, and the neighborhood of Theresienhöhe, south of which new housing developments have recently been built. The park is also meant to be a link between these new developments. Its striking design is composed of a series of containers placed in a row, alluding to the trains traveling underground. These containers are like toy boxes filled with games: a sports and play area made of rubberized tartan, a moraine formed by a lawn, and in between the two, a large expanse of sand and gravel.

The landscape cover is a generous open area accessible from all sides, which, on one hand, links the residential areas on both sides by means of imagined movement, but on the other, provides a soothing contrast to the density of the adjoining housing developments, giving a sense of being faraway while still within a busy locality.

**DESIGNERS**
Topotek 1 with Rosemarie Trockel and Catherine Venart

**CLIENT**
City of Munich

**COLLABORATORS**
Catherine Venart (architect),
Landeshauptstadt (main contractor)

**AREA**
4.2 acres (1.7 ha)

**COST**
n/a

**PHOTOGRAPHER**
Hanns Joosten

A pine grove reinforces the slightly curved
north perimeter of the track. Along both sides
of the open space, green front gardens connect
the project with the adjacent housing.

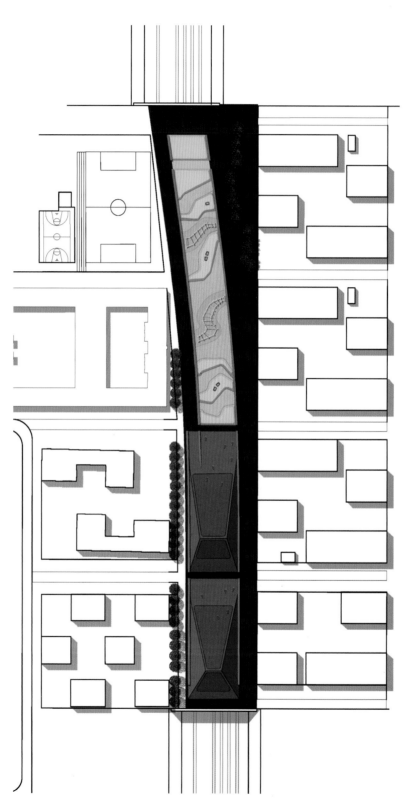

Site plan

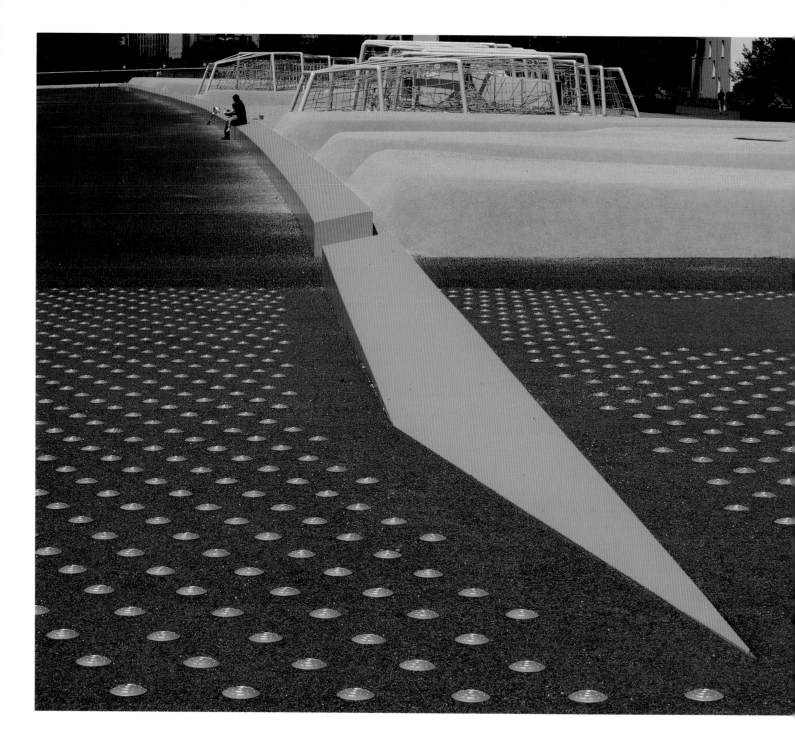

# GHOST TRAIN AMUSEMENT PARK

## Lima, Peru   2009

The project focuses on the recovery of one of the most controversial spaces in the city: a large concrete platform thirty feet wide and several miles long of what was to be Lima's new elevated electric train, but which has remained unfinished, becoming instead, part of the sad industrial landscape of the neighborhood of Surquillo.

This neglected infrastructure offered an opportunity for an alternative use. Basurama, a Spanish collective, saw on the site the potential for a much needed urban park. The community, including various local artists, was brought in to participate in the design process to transform the space into a number of attractions, making the railway infrastructure a small amusement park.

The project was developed with limited resources and reused materials such as used car parts, and bright colors were used to detract from the unsightly appearance of the dilapidated concrete structure and to make the intervention more visible.

Since its opening, the project has triggered the development of a series of similar interventions in other parts of the city, and the park has become an example of sustainability and collective work for the reactivation of derelict spaces and the increase of social awareness.

**DESIGNER**
Basurama

**CLIENT**
District of Surquillo, City of Lima

**COLLABORATORS**
Christian Luna (artist and performer), Sandra Nakamura (visual artist), Camila Bustamante (graphic designer), El Cartón (group of architecture students), Karem Bernedo (video artist), Playstationvagon y El Codo; Motivando Corazones, Fuerza Juvenil (artists) with the collaboration of the Municipality of Surquillo

**AREA**
n/a

**COST**
n/a

**PHOTOGRAPHER**
Basurama

battle space

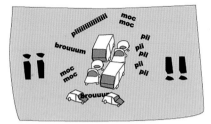

moc
moc

piiiiiiiiiiiii

brouuum

moc
moc

pii
pii pii
pii pii
pii

brouuu

¿ ? 

cars VS people

a railway line with no train!

$

Low cost project

re-used
tires

drills

ropes

people

domestic
architecture

flying
chairs

"rambo"

"toro Loco"

Programmatic diagrams

Súbete
al Tren
fantasma

Parque de Diversiones

Cómo llegar:
Vías abandonadas del Tren Eléctrico
en Azcapotzalco
desde el 30 enero 2010

EL TREN VOLADON

CANOA KRAKATOA        El Barco Pirata

Photomontage of the structure with the various attractions

Deseo    El Tren Fantasma    **EL MIRADOR**

**¡RAMBO!**    **EL TORO LOCO**    Las Sillas Voladoras

e project was conceived as a way of giving the
ace back to the children and the community.
ncludes games produced from discarded
es and other recycled materials.

# NATURE IN WALDKIRCHEN 2007
# A DECENTRALIZED EXHIBITION CONCEPT

## Waldkirchen, Germany    2007

A new urban park was developed on the southeastern edge of the old town, along the Waeschelbach creek as part of the garden exhibition that takes place annually in Waldkirchen. Through a comprehensive urban reorganization, a spacious entrance square to the urban park and to the garden exhibition was created. This is where all the main events and activities take place.

Scenic balconies with interpretive panels offer panoramic views of the Waeschelbach Valley, which features a variety of historic and natural sites like the floodplain forests and the hillside meadows along the Waeschelbach creek. The distinct meadows and the diverse landforms served as backdrops to develop different gardens and to integrate the man-made settings with the natural environment. The elements of the urban park, including the entrance square, the urban promenade, the water staircase, the cherry gardens, the pond, the creek, and the spacious meadows can stand on their own as independent interventions with distinct qualities. An additional focus of the garden exhibition is the garden "Bellevue" along the loop path. It represents the city's character and complements the other municipal open spaces like the marketplace, the cemetery, the urban park, and the sports fields.

**LANDSCAPE ARCHITECT**
Rehwaldt Landschaftsarchitekten

**LOCATION**
Waldkirchen, Germany

**CLIENT**
Natur in Waldkirchen 2007

**AREA**
18.5 acres (7.5 ha)

**COST**
USD 3,268,000 (EUR 2.4 million)

**PHOTOGRAPHER**
Rehwaldt Landschaftsarchitekten

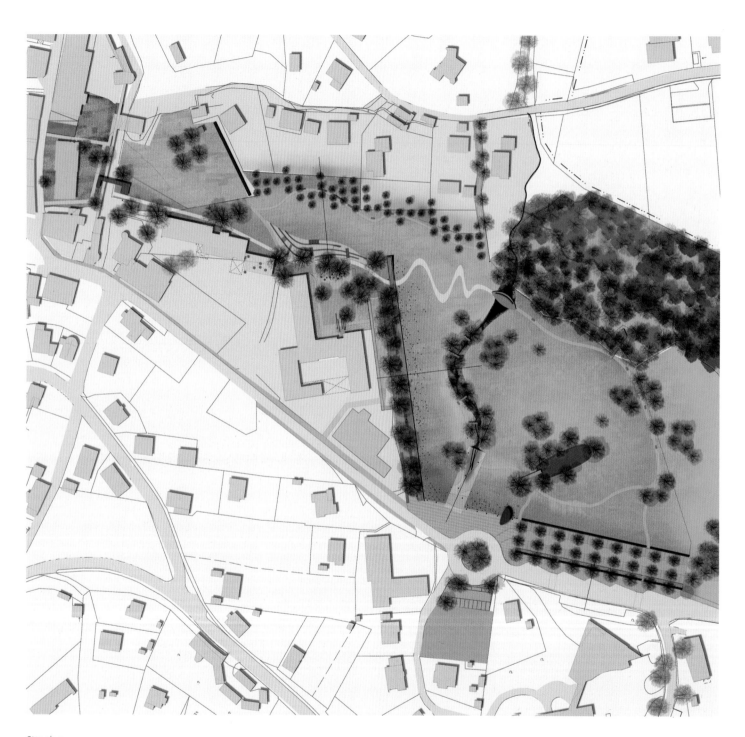

Site plan

Waterbound paths frame the shrub and bush
plantings and show the inside and outside
areas. A rectangular pond with water jets was
strategically placed overlooking the area. The
water basin is a playground and recreational zone.
The historic site of Waldkirchen´s water reserve
was interpreted anew by using the instruments
of contemporary landscape architecture.

# BURGHAUSEN AND BAVARIAN LANDESGARTENSCHAU (STATE GARDEN SHOW)

## Burghausen, Germany    2004

The city of Burghausen was aiming at the development of an urban open space system using a decentralized exhibition concept oriented toward a comprehensive view of the city. Ideas of old town, modern town, and historic castle were defined through different thematic focal points as part of a garden show, and were then functionally connected.

Today, the different areas of this garden show are integrated into the urban structure and have become part of the everyday life of the city.

Through the garden show, it was made possible to raise public interest for some "forgotten places" and reintegrate the castle into daily life. Furthermore, a great-

er support for future development was achieved.

Regained gardens along the river Salzach strengthen the attractiveness of the waterfront, linking it to the city's network of walkways.

For the first time, an interconnected urban open space system could be established, through means of the garden show. The urban park becomes an icon for the City of Burghausen. An exciting urban experience is made possible through new walkway connections and visual axes. In this regard, the activities of the garden show essentially contribute to long-term urban development and the creation of a restored image of the city.

**LANSCAPE ARCHITECT**
Rehwaldt Landschaftsarchitekten

**LOCATION**
Burghausen, Germany

**CLIENT**
Stadt Burghausen/ LGS 2004

**AREA**
55.6 acres (22.5 ha)

**COST**
USD 15,659,550 (EUR 11.5 million)

**PHOTOGRAPHER**
Rehwaldt Landschaftsarchitekten

The castle has always been used as a residence, with flower, fruit, and vegetable gardens. Some focal areas were emphasized through permanent plantings; other areas are reserved for the garden show's features.

Site plan

e garden show includes the installation of
ayground elements, such as a steep spiral
de. Respecting the demands of monument
nservation, the play structures are designed
mobile, temporary elements that can be
ocated after the garden exhibition.

# COLUMNS—ELEPHANT LANDSCAPE COPENHAGEN ZOO

## Copenhagen, Denmark 2008

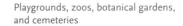

SLA has designed the landscape for Copenhagen Zoo's new elephant area. This project was in collaboration with the firm Foster + Partners, who designed a new Elephant House.

The renovation of the northern section of the zoological gardens, which includes the elephant's enclosure, eliminated the visual boundary between the zoo and Frederiksberg Park.

The elephant's new outdoor space is conceived as a dry, sandy plain with water puddles, mud holes, and concrete columns. The columns, which mainly serve as a fence between the elephants and the visitors, provide the elephants with shade during the intense summer sun and make reference to the elephant's original habitat—the Indian forest.

The new landscape surrounding Copenhagen Zoo's Elephant House has provided the elephants with better living conditions. Visitors also have more possibilities for movement around the colossal animals and can experience larger variations in surrounding space. The buildings and the landscape that constitute the elephants' enclosure add a new exotic feature to the romantic setting of Frederiksberg Gardens.

**LANDSCAPE ARCHITECT**
SLA

**CLIENT**
Copenhagen Zoo

**COLLABORATORS**
Foster & Partners, Rambøll, Buro Happold, Davis Langdon, Ultraaqua

**AREA**
2.7 acres (1.1 ha)

**COST**
USD 27.2 million (EUR 20 million)

**PHOTOGRAPHER**
SLA

Partially buried in the ground, the new Elephant
House permits the public to walk around the roof
and look down onto the elephants' indoor quarters,
which receive plenty of daylight through the glass
domes, a design signature of Foster + Partners.

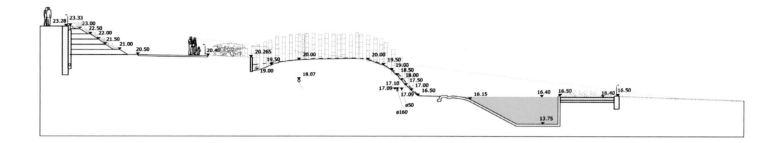

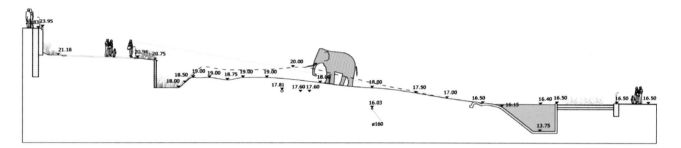

Sections

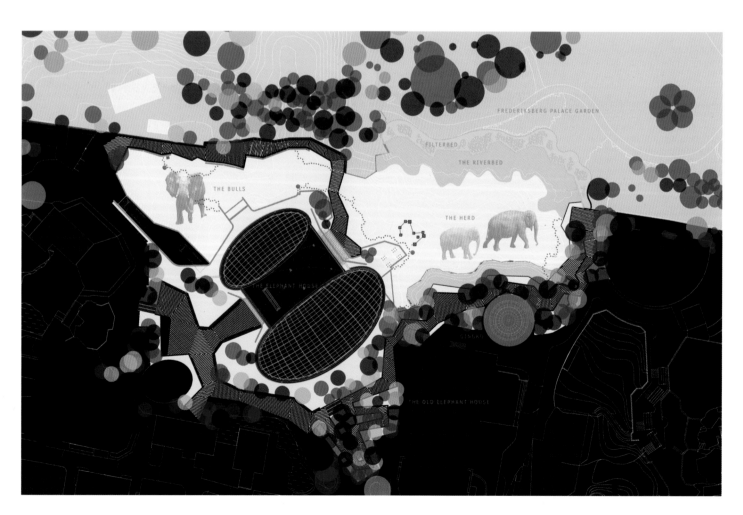

Site plan

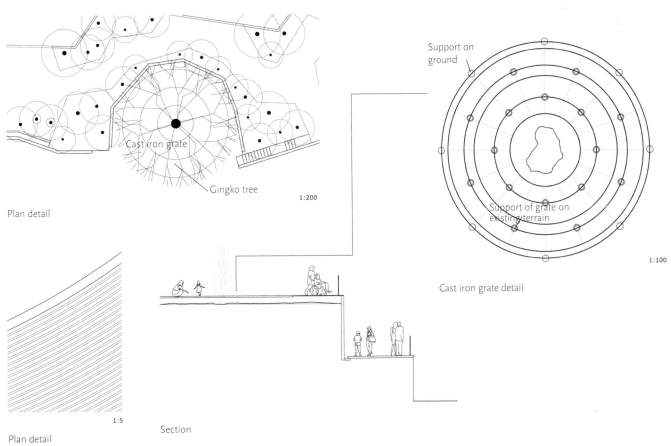

Plan detail

Cast iron grate

Gingko tree

1:200

Support on ground

Support of grate on existing terrain

1:100

Cast iron grate detail

1:5

Plan detail

Section

# WUPPERTAL ZOO

## Wuppertal, Germany    2007

A neighborhood district with a recreational focus was developed along the Wupper river with a stadium as centerpiece that happened to be located near the zoo. The project consisted of the extension and remodel of the zoological garden in combination with the redesign of the stadium's surroundings.

The intervention establishes a relationship with the Wupper river. This is achieved by the integration of the stadium's surroundings into the remodel plan and by the redesign of Hubertus Avenue to strengthen the connection between the zoo's main entrance and the Wupper river.

The zoo's character as a landscaped park has been emphasized by reshaping the existing vegetation and introducing water as a strong organizational element of the space. The Wiesenbach creek, which in some parts was flowing through underground pipes, is now exposed. The reshaping of the topography reaches its artistic form of expression through artificial rock formations to create the new predators' habitats. The visitors are taken on a journey through a rocky valley that, far from being a mere scenic backdrop, is meant to enhance physical activity and provide a more stimulating experience.

As a result, the remodel has turned the zoo into a new attraction within the city's system of urban open spaces.

**LANDSCAPE ARCHITECT**
Rehwaldt Landschaftsarchitekten

**LOCATION**
Wuppertal, Germany

**CLIENT**
Wuppertal Facility Management

**COLLABORATORS**
Rohdecan Architekten / Heinle, Wischer und Partner Architekten

**AREA**
12.6 acres (5.1 ha)

**COST**
USD 16,612,743 (EUR 12.2 million)

**PHOTOGRAPHER**
Rehwaldt Landschaftsarchitekten

An elevated lookout on a man-made rock formation,
accessible through an underground path, offers a
close look at the lions' enclosure and spectacular
views of the zoo and the adjacent natural landscape.

Site plan

e zoo entrance has been reorganized. It
placed beside the historic main building
d designed in a self-contained manner. A
ulptural new building accommodates the
ferent spatial and functional demands.

Ephemeral Lake

Mark Stoner and Edwina Kearney
2005

# THE AUSTRALIAN GARDEN

## Cranbourne, Australia    2005

The garden addresses contemporary environmental and cultural issues to bring new forms of garden experience to visitors. It enhances the tension between the natural landscape and our human urge to suppress it as a driving creative impulse for exploration, expression, and interpretation of the landscape.

Water is the mediating element between the natural and man-made gardens. Emerging at the entry of the garden, it cascades into shallow rock pools, gaining in expanse and volume until it wraps an island in the northern end. There, the natural and human influences are integrated. Along the length of the site, fingers of woodland link the natural and human influenced sides, never fully connecting. They serve as a constant visual link reminding us that each side complements the other.

The garden seeks to create an environment in which specific qualities of the landscape are highlighted in a way that will inspire visitors to further explore Australian flora.

The western side of the garden is inspired by the woodland, the sand gardens, the tree-covered hills, and the chasm and marsh gardens; the eastern side is influenced by ideas and images of a man-made environment, with highly designed exhibition gardens lining the central promenade.

**LANDSCAPE ARCHITECT**
Taylor Cullity Lethlean

**CLIENT**
Royal Botanic Gardens, Cranbourne

**COLLABORATORS**
Paul Thompson (plant design), Meinhardt (engineering), Barry Webb and Associates (lighting), Irrigation Design Consultants (irrigation), Robert Van De Graaff (soil science), Donald Cant Watts Corke (cost planning), Greg Clark with Taylor Cullity Lethlean (escarpment wall), Rockpool Waterway Waterforms International with Taylor Cullity Lethlean (water feature), Mark Stoner and Edwina Kearney (ephemeral lake sculpture)

**AREA**
61.8 acres (25 ha)

**COST**
n/a

**AWARDS**
2007 Overall Award in Landscape Architecture from the Australian Institute of Landscape Architects, Victoria Chapter; 2007 Award of Excellence in Design from the Australian Institute of Landscape Architects, Victoria Chapter

**PHOTOGRAPHER**
Taylor Cullity Lethlean, Peter Hyatt, Ben Wrigley, Dianna Snape

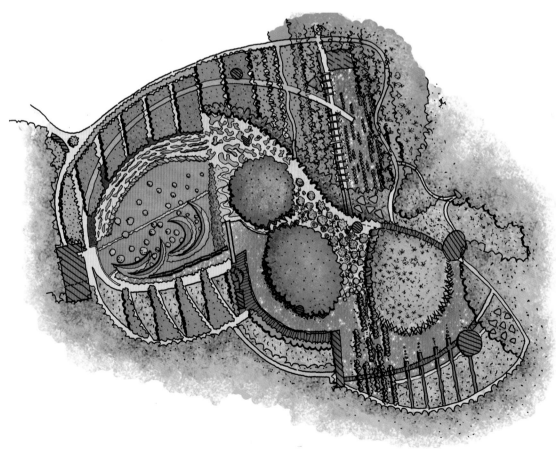

Color rendering of the Australian Garden plan

# A PLOT / MEGARON—ASSISTENS CEMETERY

## Copenhagen, Denmark   2004

To the surprise of many, Assistens Cemetery is used both as a memorial place and as a park. Located in the neighborhood of Nørrebro in Copenhagen, it has become a life-giving green lung and center of social interaction. The project was aimed to extend these social activities to the new space of A Plot / Megaron. The work consists of two parts: "A Plot" by SLA (the horizontal part) and "Megaron" (the 11.5-feet-high sculpture) by sculptor Morten Stræde. The sculpture and the slabs lying on the lawn are carved out of sandstone and granite and placed in the new area, where two axes cross each other at a perpendicular angle. It stands tall, with a light serpentine twist as a landmark and meeting point in the garden.

A Plot consists of thirty patches of either grass or red sandstone, laid into the ground in varying sizes and at different angles. Assistens Cemetery is divided into sections on a grid of 3.28 × 3.28 feet. Each space has an individual shape and design. Grass and natural stone such as sandstone and granite are the dominant materials.

The work relates to the physical dimensions of the cemetery, as well as to change and transience. The whole installation appears in different states determined by the time of year, erosion, and use, and is therefore constantly changing.

**LANDSCAPE ARCHITECT**
SLA

**LOCATION**
Copenhagen, Denmark

**COLLABORATORS**
Stine Poulsen (A Plot), Morten Stræde (Megaron) with poem by Klaus Høeck

**AREA**
4,306 sq ft (400 m²)

**COST**
USD 286,146 (EUR 210,000)

**PHOTOGRAPHER**
SLA, Torben Petersen

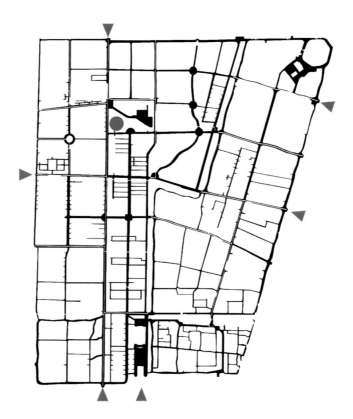

Site plan

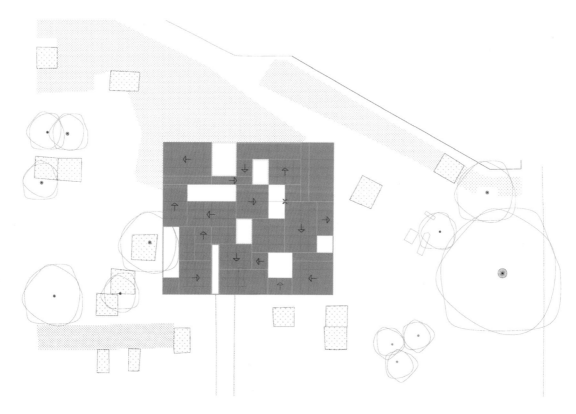

Enlarged detail plan

The sculptural called "Megaron" is meant to
change and erode over time: just like the sandstone
slabs lying on the ground, the sculpture will
acquire a patina, providing the composition
with the character of a work in progress.

The sandstone slabs rise to different levels above the lawn of the cemetery. Worth noting are the lines from a poem by Danish poet Klaus Høeck engraved on the side of three stone blocks: "What are you searching for here / where life has turned to stone / find your own death."

find din egen død

# CEMETERY IN PIEVE DI SOLIGO

Pieve di Soligo, Italy    2010

At the foot of a picturesque natural landscape near a historic city center, a small cemetery and its recent expansion (1980) are the scope of work on a formal reorganization affecting accessibility and functionality. The cemetery is formed by two systems: the first is the original installation and is characterized by an axis that links it, both physically via a footpath and visibly, to the San Martino church (a small historical church in an elevated position with respect to the cemetery); the second system is defined by the expansion.

The project is composed of simple partitions and surfaces that create a sequence of zones that lead toward the place of burial. It reinforces the entrance axis, which connects with the church by extending it to form a strip flaked by a row on both sides of *Lagerstroemia indica* trees. The strip is in turn delimited by two large expanses of lawn, creating a transitional area between the dense surroundings. To one side, a new rectangular enclosure forms a protected space that establishes a respectful distance between guests who are visiting the departed and those who are looking for a place to get away from the nearby busy road.

**ARCHITECT**
made associati_ architettura e paesaggio

**CLIENT**
Comune di Pieve di Soligo

**COLLABORATORS**
Massimo Galeotti

**AREA**
107,639 sq ft (10.000 m²)

**COST**
n/a

**PHOTOGRAPHER**
Adriano Marangon

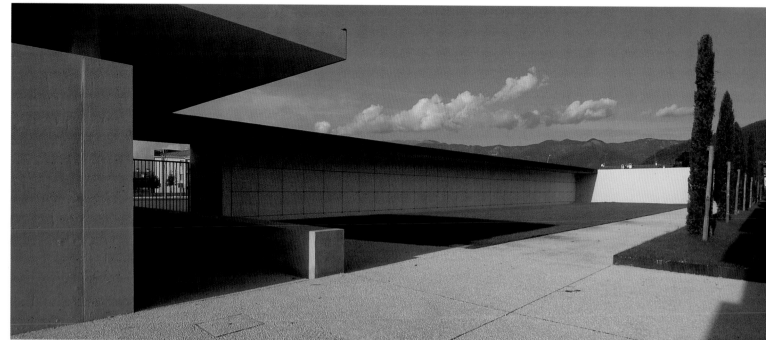

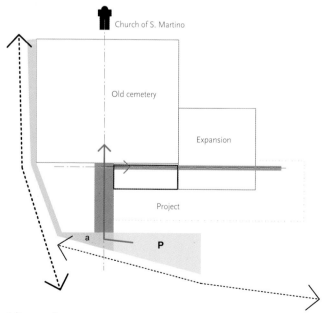

Church of S. Martino

Old cemetery

Expansion

Project

a

P

Adjacency diagram

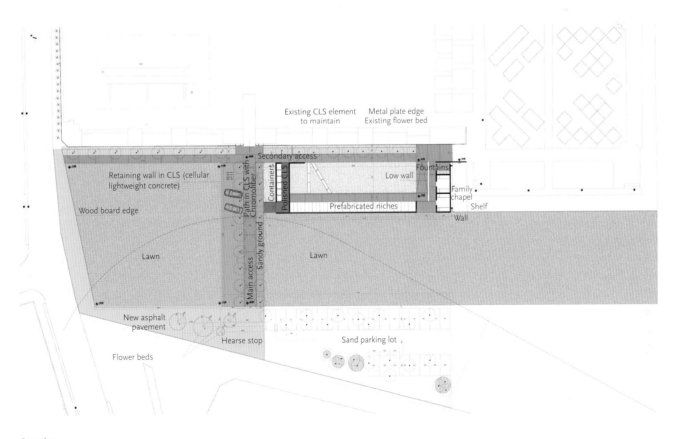

Existing CLS element    Metal plate edge
to maintain    Existing flower bed

Secondary access

Containers

Path in CLS with Chromohber

Polished CLS

Retaining wall in CLS (cellular lightweight concrete)

Low wall

Fountains

Family chapel

Wood board edge

Prefabricated niches

Shelf

Wall

Main access

Sandy ground

Lawn

Lawn

New asphalt pavement

Hearse stop

Sand parking lot

Flower beds

Site plan

# DE OOSTERVAART CEMETERY

## Zuid-Scharwoude, the Netherlands    2009

The new De Oostervaart cemetery is part of a large green area in the municipality of Langedijk. The program required that the cemetery would be integrated with a recreational area, a sports field, and allotment gardens.

The cemetery is divided into small grave fields linked by a network of paths. These paths are defined by lawns, soft mounds, and widely spread trees and connect the different fields that constitute the cemetery while also linking the cemetery with the park. The presence of water defines the landscape where a pond and the region's characteristic straight-edged watercourses take center stage. This dictated the design of the cemetery, which, for technical reasons, had to be constructed above water level. Seven "grave chambers," distributed throughout the site and built at different heights depending on the water level, were designed following different approaches that involved the planting of various plant and tree species and the specific placement of gravestones. A unifying element in the design is the border of high hedges around these "grave chambers," providing intimacy.

**LANDSCAPE ARCHITECT**
Karres en Brands landschapsarchitecten

**CLIENT**
Municipality of Langedijk

**COLLABORATORS**
Onix architects (waiting room and maintenance room design), Rod'or Technical Advice Bureau (construction)

**AREA**
Cemetery total 14.8 acres (6 hectares), 1st phase 6.7 acres (2.7 hectares)

**COST**
USD 1.6 million (EUR 1.2 million)

**PHOTOGRAPHER**
Karres en Brands landschapsarchitecten

The path system establishes connections between the grave fields and their surroundings, which are part of the adjacent recreational area, while visual relationships among the different areas are facilitated by viewpoints and stairways.

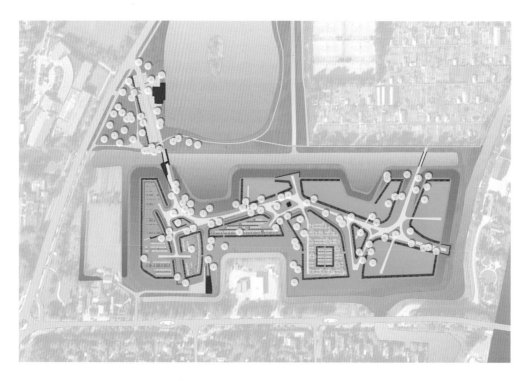

Site plan

# DE NIEUWE OOSTER AMSTERDAM

Amsterdam, the Netherlands    2007

De Nieuwe Ooster cemetery and crematorium is the largest of its kind in the Netherlands. It was built in three phases—in 1889, 1915, and 1928—and has undergone various subsequent changes. In 2001, a renovation process began and two years later, the cemetery became a national monument. The first and second phases, designed by Leonard Springer, present a unified spatial quality. The third phase, however, stands out for the lack of this unity due to various interventions. The project, which focuses on the area developed during this third phase, accommodates the existing burial areas as well as the framework for an extension. It is intended to confer the site with a new identity. To achieve this goal, a bold but relatively easy to implement intervention was developed. The design consists of a series of parallel strips, some of which are planted with hedges to create different compartmentalized areas. It incorporates two distinct zones: Section 65, which includes rows of stone slabs slightly raised from the ground; and Section 87 where a long and narrow pond and an urn wall accentuate the linearity of the design. The overall area is punctuated with loosely planted birch trees that serve as a unifying element of the design.

**LANDSCAPE ARCHITECT**
Karres en Brands Landschapsarchitecten

**LOCATION**
Amsterdam, the Netherlands

**CLIENT**
De Nieuwe Ooster begraafplaats, crematorium en gedenkpark

**COLLABORATORS**
Maria van Kesteren (design charons in pond), Rod'or Technical Advice Bureau (construction)

**AREA**
2.47 acres (2 ha)

**COST**
USD 2,180,160 (EUR 1,600,000)

**AWARDS**
Topos Award (2004), 2nd Prize
Torsoloranzo Award (2006), 1st Prize
Rheinzink Award (2008)

**PHOTOGRAPHER**
Karres en Brands, Jeroen Musch, Thyra Brandt

The design approach for the redefinition of the cemetery's different zones is based on linearity. Long rows of stone slabs demarcate the graves without any prime locations as an expression of equality, providing homogeneity while maintaining the particular character of each zone.

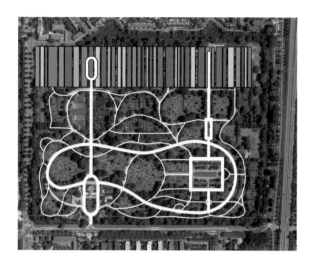

Conceptual plan of scope of work

Conceptual plan of the three different areas

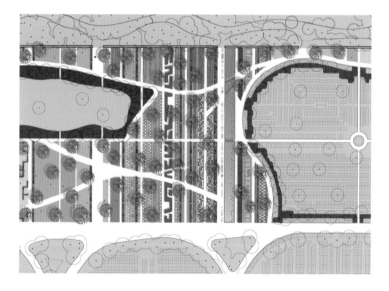

Plan detail of Section 87

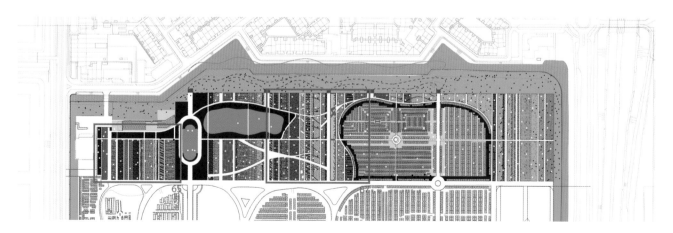

General plan of Section 65 and Section 87

ther than connecting the three different areas of
cemetery, the design distinguishes each of the
nes—enhancing their own spatial qualities.

The area developed in the third phase and the object of the project accommodates the existing burial areas and the Garden of Remembrance.

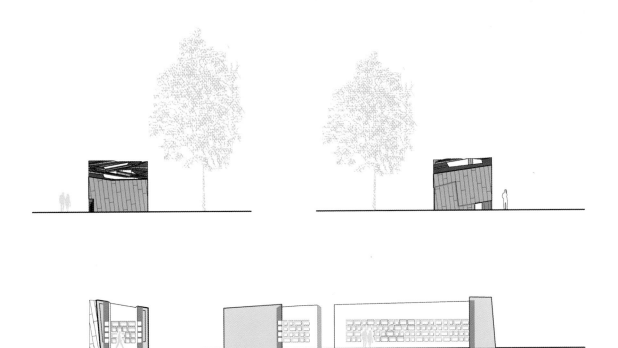

Elevations at urn wall

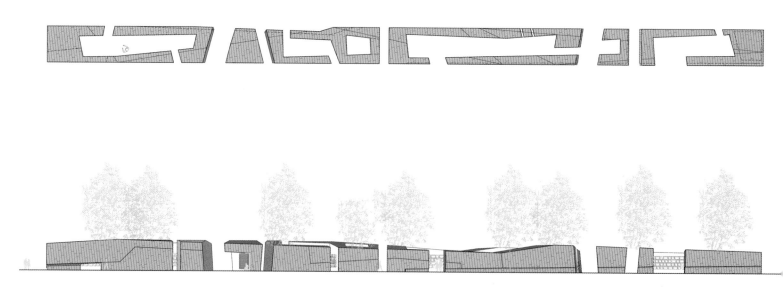

Elevations at urn wall

# INFRASTRUCTURE
# DEVELOPMENTS

# ELECTRIC RAMPS IN THE HISTORIC CENTER OF VITORIA-GASTEIZ

## Vitoria-Gasteiz, Spain    2007

The historical district of Vitoria-Gasteiz sits on a small hill. The city's steep topography has made any changes difficult, and its structure has remained intact throughout history. Nonetheless, the city center has become isolated from the rest of the city and ghettos have formed. A thorough accessibility study was the base of the project, which consists of covered mechanical ramps. The decision to cover the ramps guaranteed their use given the extreme winter conditions in this northern Spanish city, the second largest in the Basque country. This keeps the snow and the ice off the surface of the ramps. Also, the architect wanted to avoid the me-chanical look, and by covering the ramps he succeeds in bringing more attention to the envelop of the ramps as an architectural element. The project is simple and complex simultaneously. Its simplicity lies in the successive repetition of a stainless steel frame. The panes of tempered glass that constitute the envelop of the structure are also identical. The project's complexity is in its three-dimensional perception. The repetition of the same element works like a sequence of frames in a film. The composition takes, then, a higher level of complexity by means of short revolving movements around the ramp's long axis.

**ARCHITECT**
Roberto Ercilla Arquitectura

**COLLABORATORS**
Iñaki Ciganda, Laura Angulo, Raquel Ochoa, Teresa Artola (design); Agustín de la Tajada (quantity surveyor); Eduardo Martín (structural engineer); Proiekt, (stainless steel); EBA (construction)

**AREA**
n/a

**COST**
USD 5,021,800 (EUR 3,685,475)

**PHOTOGRAPHER**
César San Millán

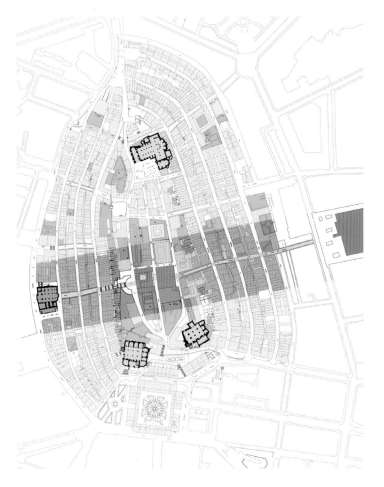

Location map

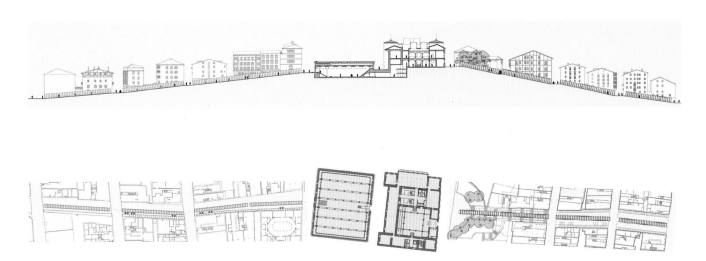

Site plan and section

The sensation of rotational movement that the user perceives is emphasized by the continuous sliding movement of the ramp and the view of the immediate surroundings through the glass envelop.

# ENTRANCE AND TRANSFER ACCELERATOR OVERVECHT STATION

## Utrecht, the Netherlands    2011

The entrance of the Overvecht Station built in 1985 had fallen into a state of disrepair in spite of extensive maintenance. Its dilapidated appearance and its outdated design triggered the decision to revamp the area, which functions as a link between two neighborhoods and as an entrance to the railway system. HIK Ontwerpers first presented the idea to ProRail, the government agency responsible for the maintenance and organization of the Dutch railway system, as a solution to give the station a more playful character and detract from the area's unsightly appearance.

The HIK design team proposed adding public functions and fun in order to bestow the place with character. The new design is meant to make commuters and visitors feel comfortable when walking through the station entrance. It is also a meeting place and a pleasant spot to eat lunch and wait for the train.

To soften the hard character of the station, HIK has added a playful layer composed of amphitheater steps, plants, and a slide. This slide attracts children, along with their parents who sit on the steps for a moment while waiting for the next train.

**ARCHITECT**
HIK Ontwerpers

**LOCATION**
Utrecht, the Netherlands

**CLIENT**
NS / ProRail

**COLLABORATORS**
HEMUBO Concrete Technology

**AREA**
4,950 sq ft (460 m²)

**COST**
USD 340,650 (EUR 250,000)

**PHOTOGRAPHER**
HIK Ontwerpers

Axonometric view of the Overvecht Station entrance amphitheater

roRail, the Dutch railway maintenance
ompany, hired HIK Ontwerpers to redesign
e station to improve its safety and usability.
spired by amphitheaters, the designers
built the stairs and added vegetation.

The Transfer Accelerator is a slide that children
and adults alike can use to reach the bottom of
the stairs faster. But more importantly, it is also
a playful urban intervention that has generated
positive spin for the neighborhood of Overvecht.

# ARGANZUELA FOOTBRIDGE

Madrid, Spain   2010

The opening of a new park on the east bank of the Manzanares River and the burying of the highway that ran along its edges provided for the creation of the Arganzuela footbridge. It was designed to link the neighborhoods on the right and left banks of the river. The bridge, which is for both pedestrians and cyclists, also provides direct access to the park below. Structurally supported by two pillars at each end, the footbridge seems to hover in midair over the river. It is formed by two helicoidal shapes expanding from 16 to 39 feet in diameter and wrapped in a metallic mesh that shelters the interior space from extreme weather and provides a dynamic experience for the users. The two cones, which together measure over 820 feet, meet on the east side of the river at a small hill, also the high point of the bridge. There, their wide ends rest on a knoll that makes for a vista point over the park and the surrounding city. From this exceptional location, it is possible to admire the famous Toledo Bridge. Spaced wooden slats make up the floor of the bridge to reinforce the lightweight quality of the construction and to allow the sunlight to penetrate through to the park below. Shaded during the day, the footbridge becomes luminous at night.

**ARCHITECT**
Dominique Perrault Architecture

**LOCATION**
Madrid, Spain

**CLIENT**
Madrid City Council, Madrid, Spain

**COLLABORATORS**
MC2 / Julio Martínez Calzón, Madrid (structure); TYPSA, Madrid (mechanical engineering)

**COMPLETION DATE**
2010

**AREA**
24.7 acres (10 ha); footbridge 492 ft (150 m) (section 1), 420 ft (128 m) (section 2) length, 16 to 39 ft width

(5 to 12 m)

**COST**
n/a

**PHOTOGRAPHER**
Georges-Fessy, Gaelle-Lauriot-Prevost

Footbridge elevation

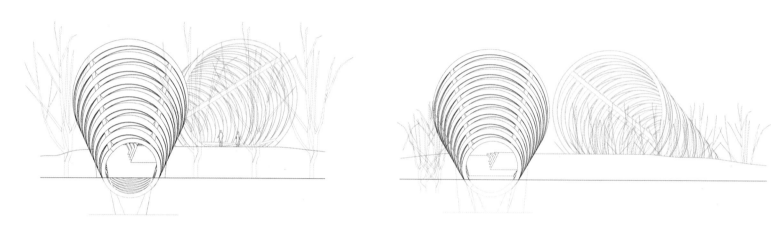

Elevations at vista point

Site plan

part of the Madrid Rio Project, a new linear
rk along the river covers an unsightly highway.
is park and various bridges are part of a
ogram to reconnect the city center with the
ighborhoods on the other side of the river.

Mesh

Mesh support
structure (ribs)

Main structure

Pillars    Joints    Diagonals    Ties (longitudinal
(spiral structure)    structure)

Base

Footbridge North    Footbridge Route

Diagram of the bridge make up

e knoll in the park is the meeting place of the
o wide ends of the cones and a direct access
int to the park, which includes bicycle paths,
aygrounds, urban beaches, and new planted areas.

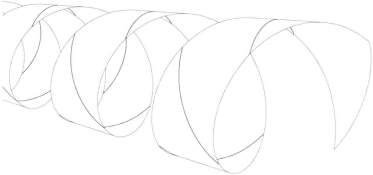

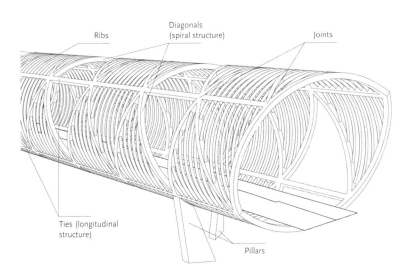

Ribs

Diagonals
(spiral structure)

Joints

Ties (longitudinal
structure)

Pillars

Partial axonometric view

The stainless steel mesh fulfills an aesthetic and utilitarian function: it offers the users a dynamic visual experience and protects the interior from the harsh summer sunlight. At moments, the mesh offers intervals of complete transparency to enjoy the views.

# I-35 W ST. ANTHONY FALLS BRIDGE

## Minneapolis, MN, USA 2008

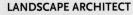

The landscape development of the site was particularly challenging due to the presence of strong features such as bridges, waterfalls, locks and dams, and river traffic. This situation guided the design toward a simple approach so as not to compete for attention. Therefore, the beauty of the project lays in the use of simple and natural materials and the planting of species that require little maintenance. The plants have been selected for their hardiness, texture, year-round interest, and their compatibility with the riparian environment.

The design is formed by three elements: the riverbank plazas, the gateway monuments, and the walls. The project is aimed to draw people to the water's edge, which is conceived as a new public space, accessible through ramps that zigzag down to the base of the arching bridge piers. The gateway monuments are represented by an inverted symbol for water—a simple message and form that animates the design of the bridge.

Stone-filled gabions face the embankment walls on both sides of the River. The selected stone was locally quarried and the gabion baskets were designed to best complement the nearby limestone outcrops and architecture.

**LANDSCAPE ARCHITECT**
Oslund and Associates

**CLIENT**
Minnesota Department
of Transportation

**COLLABORATORS**
FIGG Engineering Group (designer),
Flatiron-Manson Joint Venture (main
contractor), TKDA (civil engineer)

**AREA**
189 ft wide, 1,216 ft long

**COST**
USD 234 million

**PHOTOGRAPHER**
Oslund and Associates

3rd & I-35 Bridge

1st I-35 Bridge

Artist's impressions

Englemann ivy, a Minnesota native was used on Greenscreen®—a three-dimensional, welded wire trellising system—to cover a concrete abutment wall and anti-icing pump house on the north bank. This treatment adds green to the landscape, while also cooling these surfaces in the summer.

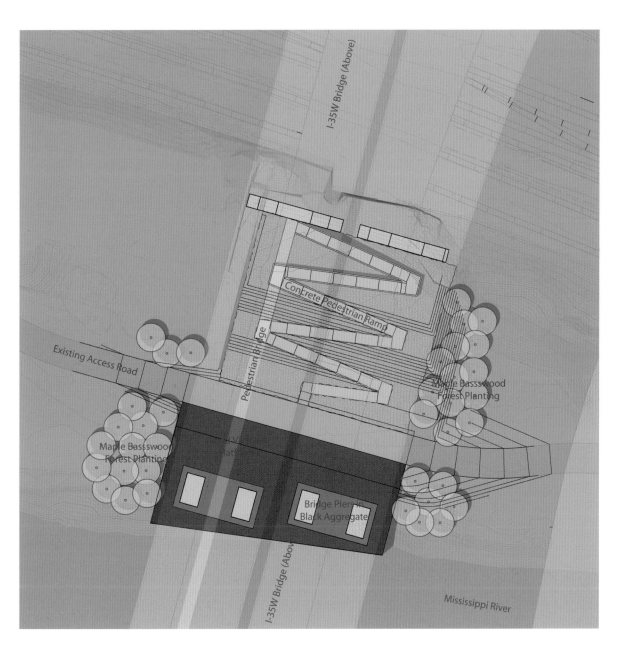

North edge improvements plan of the I-35W Bridge

Natural materials such as stone and wood integrate
the man-made intervention into the native river gorge
environment, while elements like metal gabions
remind the viewer of the river's industrial heritage.

# CRAIGIEBURN BYPASS

## Melbourne, Australia    2005

The winning plan of a competition that called for the design of an entrance to Melbourne comprises the planning and documentation of a noise-attenuation system, pedestrian bridges, and architectural features.

This project covers a three-mile stretch of highway that passes between two distinct conditions: the Craigieburn grasslands and the expanding urban limits. The design, which expresses the relationship between the freeway and these two distinct conditions, is likened to a snake shedding its skin.

Two walls were developed, each very distinctive and responding to their adjacent condition. The Curtain Wall, a long sinuous steel ribbon, is fluid and dynamic in its form. It progressively transforms along its length from a lightweight screen to a sculpted landform and ultimately into a pedestrian bridge that frames the view of the City of Melbourne. By contrast, the Scrim Wall, located alongside the residential interface, is composed of patterned acrylic panels and vertical louvers. This material provides translucency while the sequence of louvers, slightly rotated at an angle, creates a constantly changing driving experience.

**LANDSCAPE ARCHITECT**
Taylor Cullity Lethlean

**CLIENT**
VicRoads

**COLLABORATORS**
Tonkin Zulaikha Greer, Robert Owen (adjunct professor at RMIT), Meinhardt (structural engineer), Webbs (lighting), DCWC (cost planning), Bassetts (acoustics), Nexus Landscape Consultants (VRML), VicRoads (landscape design), Abi Group (civil construction), Eco Dynamic (landscape construction)

**AREA**
3 miles (4.8 km)

**COST**
USD 29.8 million (Aus$ 30 million)

**AWARDS**
2006 Award for Excellence in Design from the Australian Institute of Landscape Architects (AILA)

**PHOTOGRAPHER**
Taylor Cullity Lethlean, John Gollings, Peter Hyatt

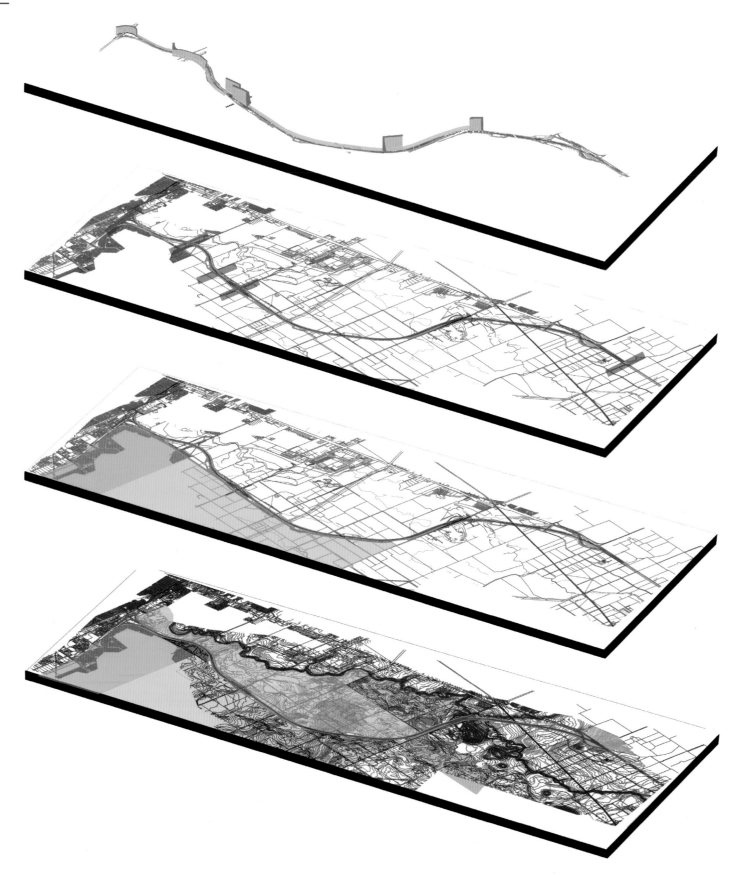

Relationship diagrams between the project's elements and its various adjacent conditions

Artist's rendition of Craigieburn bypass

night, the Scrim Wall is subtly illuminated,
ansforming the intensity of traffic via
ectrical impulses to become an ephemeral
owing architecture of light.

# SEAFRONT AND RIVERBANK RECUPERATION

# CHONGAE CANAL SOURCE POINT PARK—A SUNKEN STONE GARDEN

## Seoul, South Korea    2005

The ChonGae Sunken Stone Garden is a seven-mile canal project consisting of the redevelopment of this highly polluted canal in the business and commercial city of Seoul. The concept for the project is a symbolic representation of the imagined future reunification of North and South Korea. The work included the demolition of nearly four miles of an elevated highway that covered the canal and divided the city. With the intent to create a pedestrian-focused environment, Mikyoung Kim worked closely with local landscape architects and the U.S. Army Corps of Engineers to mitigate the effects of water contamination.

The design was guided by the canal's varying water levels at different times of the day and at different seasons, while taking into account the important floods that occur during South Korea's monsoon season. Storm water runoff is harvested and enters the ChonGae canal, while sewage is diverted into a separate purification system. Mikyoung Kim designed two of the various stepped stone blocks that permit the reading of the different water levels and encourage public engagement with the river. This urban space has become a gathering point that attracts crowds for events such as the traditional New Year's festivals, political rallies, fashion shows, and concerts where the Sunken Stone Garden gets redefined in inventive ways.

**LANDSCAPE ARCHITECT**
Mikyoung Kim Design

**CLIENT**
Seoul Metropolitan Government

**COLLABORATORS**
SeoAhn Total Landscape (Korean Landscape Architect & Landscape Contractor), Aqua-tech (fountain), Rainbow Engineering (irrigation), KECC Engineering (structural engineer), CheongSuk Engineering (structural engineer), Suenghoi Kim (bridge and walls), Crerux, Seam Lighting (lighting)

**AREA**
n/a

**COST**
n/a

**AWARDS**
Honor Award in the General Design Category from the American Society of Landscape Architects

**PHOTOGRAPHER**
Taeoh Kim

Location map

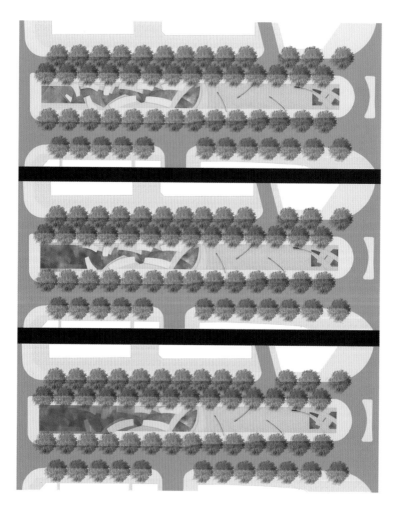

Water levels plan

Aerial perspective

e ChonGae Canal Project represents the
ne provinces through nine sources of water.
egional stone quarried from each of the nine
eas and nine source points of water were used
the collaborative restoration of the canal.

# SAMPLING GARDENS: THE TIANJIN QIAOYUAN PARK

## Tianjin City, China   2008

In the northern coastal city of Tianjin, a former shooting range and wasteland was submitted to a regeneration process with the objective of creating a 54.4-acres-urban park in response to the residents' call for environmental improvement. The new park was to include services for the city such as containing and purifying urban storm water, improving the saline-alkali soil through natural process, recovering local vegetation, and providing opportunities for environmental education.

A regenerative strategy was conceived, inspired by the adaptive vegetation of the region. The plan consisted of digging 21 cavities, both below ground level and on top of mounds. During the rainy season and due to the shallow underground water, some cavities turn into water ponds, some into wetlands, some into seasonal pools, and some stay dry. Wood platforms built in the cavities allow visitors to enjoy the site, while a network of paths guide them through the different habitats. Along these paths are information panels about natural patterns, processes, and the native species. The project defines a landscape in continuous evolution, exposing the beauty and biodiversity of a low-maintenance natural environment.

**LANDSCAPE ARCHITECT**
Turenscape

**CLIENT**
Environment construction and Investment Co. Ltd., Tianjin City

**COLLABORATORS**
Peking University Graduate School of Landscape Architecture

**AREA**
54.4 acres (22 ha)

**AWARDS**
2010 Honor Award in the General Design Category from the American Society of Landscape Architects

**PHOTOGRAPHER**
Kongjian Yu, Turenscape

1. Entrance
2. The buffer zone
3. The plant community sampling zone
4. Terrace and "savanna" zone
5. Amphitheater
6. Wetland and lake zone
7. Terrace / sunken garden zone
8. Service zone (buildings for restaurants and bars)
9. Main entrance
10. Tree belt

Spatial diagram

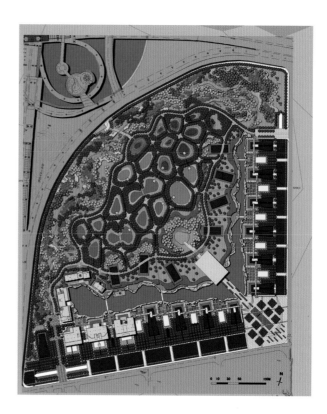

Site plan

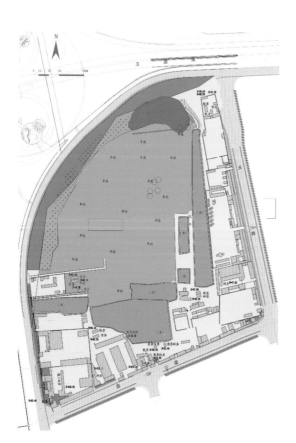

Existing conditions plan

Elevations plan

The regional landscape was once rich in wetlands and salt marshes, which have been mostly destroyed by decades of urban development. The regeneration process includes ground cover, as well as wetland vegetation that adapts to the saline-alkali soil.

The creation of new habitants started with the sowing of mixed plant species that resulted in patches of unique vegetation, while native species were allowed to grow wherever suitable.

# THE RED RIBBON—TANGHE RIVER PARK

Qinhuangdao City, Hebei Province, China   2006

The Red Ribbon—Tanghe River Park is located on the east urban border of Qinhuangdao City, in the Hebei Province of China. The site, a long corridor along the river, was covered with lush vegetation but also was a garbage dump with deserted slums, irrigation ditches, and water towers that were built for farming. Safety was also an issue since the site was practically inaccessible. As part of the urban development plan of the area, the site was considered for recreational use. The main goal was to find a design strategy that would help preserve the wildlife while providing recreational and educational functions.

Various architectural elements, including a "red ribbon" and four pavilions, were designed to organize the formerly unkempt and inaccessible site. The "red ribbon," which is made of steel fiber, integrates multiple functions and connects the various natural vegetation types concentrated in different landscape patches.

As a result, the former garbage dump has been transformed into an attraction for the residents of the nearby neighborhoods. It has been effectively developed while keeping the ecological processes of the site unaltered.

**LANDSCAPE ARCHITECT**
Turenscape

**CLIENT**
The Landscape Bureau

**COLLABORATORS**
Beijing University Graduate School of Landscape Architecture

**AREA**
49.4 acres (20 ha)

**COST**
n/a

**AWARDS**
2007 Honor Award in the General Design Category from the American Society of Landscape Architects

**PHOTOGRAPHER**
Kongjian Yu and Cao Yang

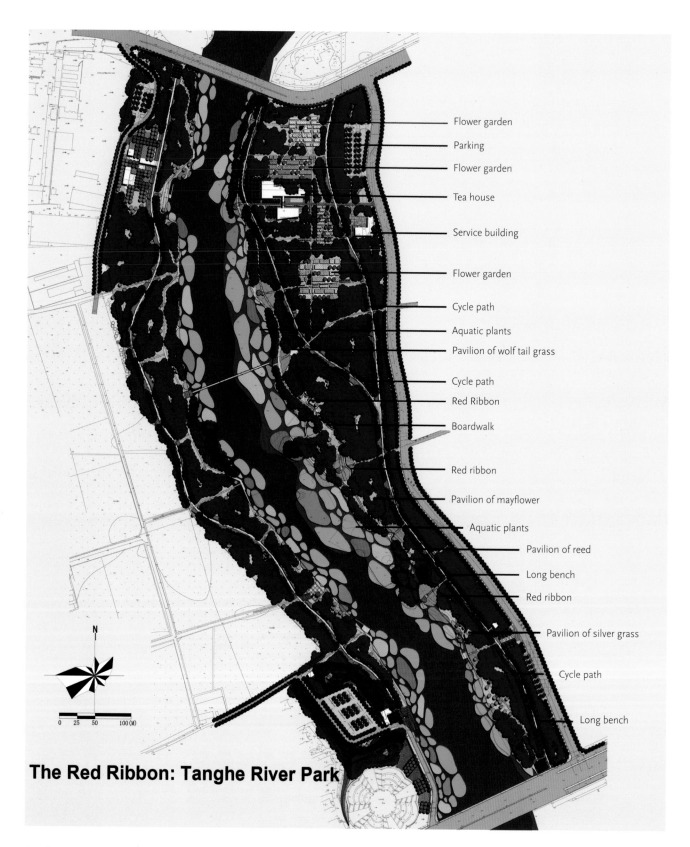

Flower garden

Parking

Flower garden

Tea house

Service building

Flower garden

Cycle path

Aquatic plants

Pavilion of wolf tail grass

Cycle path

Red Ribbon

Boardwalk

Red ribbon

Pavilion of mayflower

Aquatic plants

Pavilion of reed

Long bench

Red ribbon

Pavilion of silver grass

Cycle path

Long bench

N

0   25   50      100 (M)

## The Red Ribbon: Tanghe River Park

Site plan

Bird's-eye view rendering

, "red ribbon" was designed against the natural
ackground. It stretches 500 meters along the
verbank, integrating a boardwalk, lighting, seating,
nvironmental interpretation, and orientation.

Four pavilions in the shape of clouds and named after native grasses are distributed along the ribbon. They provide protection from the weather, serve as meeting points, and become attractions in the open fields.

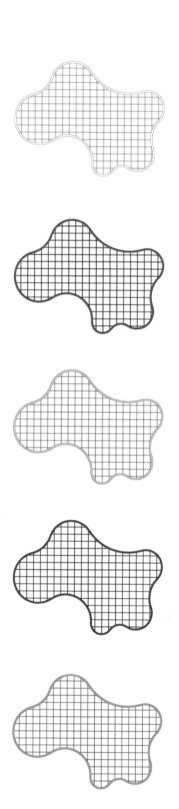

Diagrams of two of the four steel pavilions

# THE FLOATING GARDENS—YONGNING RIVER PARK

## Taizhou City, Zhejiang Province, China    2004

The existing conditions prior to the development carried out by Turenscape presented concrete embankments as part of the local flood control policy. The program of the new project had to provide alternative flood control and storm water management as a model for the entire river valley. Also, it had to provide a design scheme accessible both to locals and tourists.

The park is composed of two overlaid layers: the natural matrix and the human matrix. This design strategy generated the "Floating Gardens."

The natural matrix is composed of a wetland and vegetation necessary for the typical process of flooding and the creation of habitats. On top of this natural matrix, the "gardens of humanity" float, composed of a grid of native trees, a network of paths that connects the urban fabric with the park, as well as story boxes that allude to the culture and history of the native land and people.

A study of the flood security patterns was critical for the design of the park. This led to the restoration of a riparian wetland along the flood plain and a lake outside the river bank, both accessible to the public.

The overall project demonstrates an ecological approach to flood control and storm water management, and a high valuation of the native plants, which are often neglected.

**LANDSCAPE ARCHITECT**
Turenscape

**CLIENT**
The Government of Huangyan District, Taizhou City

**COLLABORATORS**
Beijin University Graduate School of Landscape Architecture

**AREA**
51.9 acres (21 ha)

**COST**
n/a

**AWARDS**
2006 Honor Award in the General Design Category from the American Society of Landscape Architects

**PHOTOGRAPHER**
Kongjian Yu

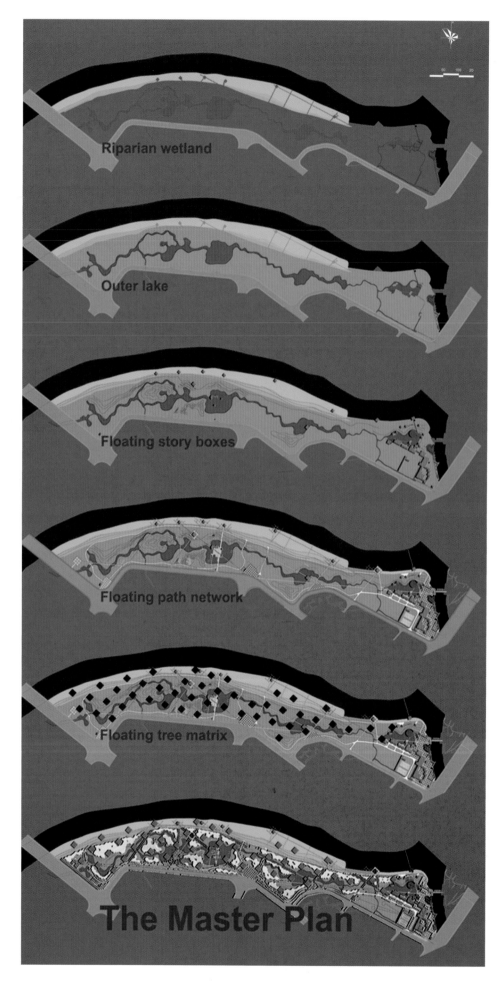

Riparian wetland

Outer lake

Floating story boxes

Floating path network

Floating tree matrix

The Master Plan

Master plan

ative grasses are used to consolidate the riverbank
d promote the integration of the design with the
rrounding ecosystem, while a network of bridges
d paths over the man-made wetland provides
formation about the area and its environment.

square floating above the man-made wetland allows
ater to flow underneath during the flooding season.
teahouse, in dialogue with the natural environment,
fers the possibility to enjoy the site year-round.

# BAY SHIP AND YACHT COMPANY

## Alameda, CA, USA   2008

This project serves as an extension and meeting point of the Bay Trail, part of what will be a 500-mile network of bicycle and walking trails connecting forty-seven cities throughout the San Francisco Bay Area. This section begins at the Alameda Ferry station and continues through an industrial corridor, along the property of the Bay Ship and Yacht Company.

A plaza was created near the ferry terminal to serve as an entry point for this section of the Bay Trail, oriented at an angle to provide views of the Oakland estuary and the San Francisco Bay. Relics from the shipping industry were collected from the shipyard and have been repurposed as key elements in the landscape, reflecting the industrial history of the site.

Planting along the trail was kept simple, with native grasses set in linear patterns that reinforce the geometry of the plaza. This low planting allows views of the water to be maintained and is in keeping with the industrial nature of the site. Plants were selected that would allow them to flourish without the need for irrigation, reducing water demand on-site. In addition, these plant materials along the edge of the site allow for the water to be filtered before entering the bay.

**DESIGNERS**
estudioOCA / Omg

**LOCATION**
Alameda, CA, USA

**CLIENT**
Bay Ship and Yacht Company

**AREA**
26,910 sq ft (2,500 m²)

**COST**
n/a

**PHOTOGRAPHER**
Bryan Cantwell

Refinished I beams function as seating, providing views of the bay. An anchor sits at the corner of the plaza, with its attached chain acting as guardrail. A pair of davits marks the gateway to the new extension of the trail.

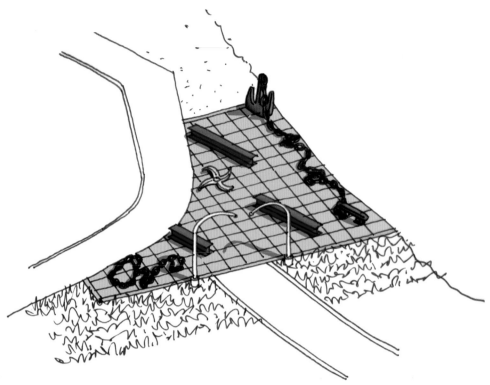

Detailed site plan of the square

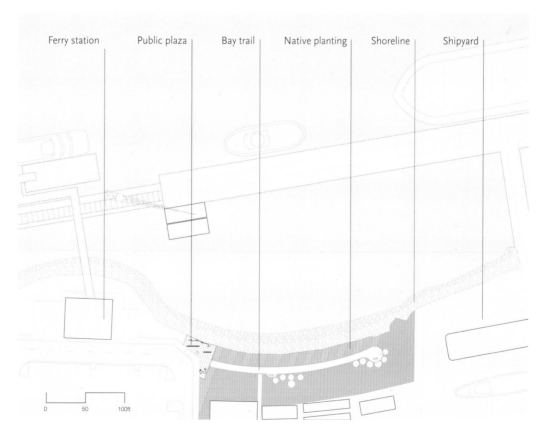

| Ferry station | Public plaza | Bay trail | Native planting | Shoreline | Shipyard |
|---|---|---|---|---|---|

0    50    100ft

Site plan

# THE NEW PARK AT THE FORMER WATER POLICE SITE

## Sydney, Australia   2009

The new park at the former Water Police site transforms a fenced-off postindustrial concrete slab into a richly varied urban waterfront parkland and building ensemble. The streets surrounding the park have been recalibrated and reduced in width. They contain significant water-sensitive environmental design via "rain gardens," which have a positive environmental and urban impact on the streetscape and design of the site. The site's restoration into public ownership as a public parkland is an important outcome for Sydney, where large extents of harborfront property is privately owned with little or no direct access to the water.

The park design is founded on an exhaustive analysis process, which traced the natural patterns, changing shoreline, and history of the urban development in the Pyrmont Peninsula. The plan creates a flexible park structure that allows for a variety of uses and maximum flexibility, including cultural events, performances, festivals, community gatherings, and exhibitions.

The most dramatic and significant component of the new park is the reinstatement of the site of a harbor beachfront that had been filled during successive industrial developments.

**LANDSCAPE ARCHITECT**
ASPECT Studios

**CLIENT**
City of Sydney Council

**COLLABORATORS**
Hill Thalis Architecture + Urban Projects (architects), CAB Consulting (landscape architect/heritage of master plan), Fiona Robbe (playground consultant), Ford Civil Contractors (head contractors), Connell Wagner (structural, civil, drainage, hydraulic engineering), TLB Engineers (marine engineering), Warwick Donnelly (playground engineering), Ecological Engineering (water sensitive urban design strategy), Deuce Design (interpretative design), Lighting, HydroPlan (irrigation), Art + Science (lighting), The People for Places + Spaces

**AREA**
44.5 acres (1.8 ha)

**COST**
USD 25.8 million (Aus$ 26 million)

**AWARDS**
NSW 2007 Award for excellence in planning form the Australian Institute of Landscape Architects, 2009 Certificate of Recognition, NSW Play Space Winner for the Parks and leisure Association, Australia Awards, CCAA Public Domain Awards 2009, Winner of Precincts, State Winner NSW, Winner Best Overall Project

**PHOTOGRAPHER**
Florian Groehn

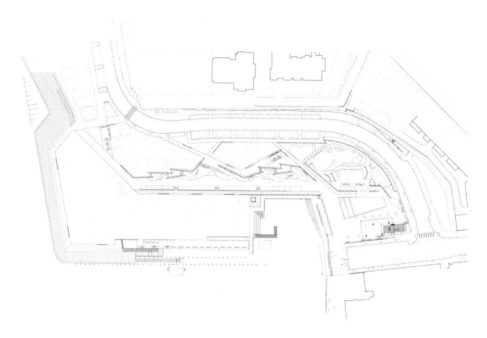

Site plan

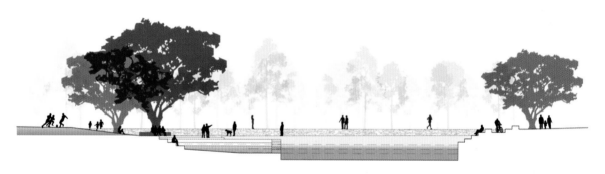

Section A

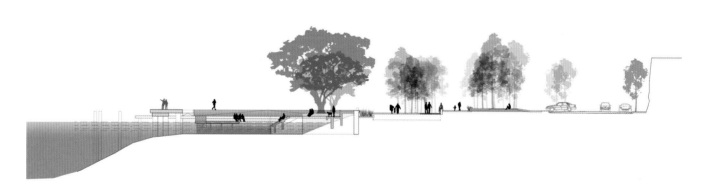

Section B

From the industrial era, the design retains
most of the seawall, the first row of piers and
headstocks, a concrete wall—located in the center
of the site—and the sandstone embankment.

Key to the structure of the new park is the foreshore promenade, which is designed along the alignment of the historic shoreline. A series of sinuous walls define the eastern boundary of the shoreline walk, and stairs allow for a variety of access points.

Recycled materials have been utilized wherever possible. Timber from existing piles has been recycled and reused on benches and walls on the site, and other excavated material has been retained when feasible.

# LUMINOUS MASTS

## Chattanooga, TN, USA  2005

Seven light masts form a row along Chattanooga's river pier as part of the city's waterfront revitalization plan. Conceptually, the masts are an extension of the pier's piling, glowing cylinders of light that appear to continue through the pier as their shadows are cast on the surface of the pier. Made of welded stainless steel wire, the masts contain reflectors formed by mirror-polished stainless steel slats that filter and redirect light to capture the quality of the light generated by the Tennessee River. Specifically, the slats are staggered to maintain transparency and oriented so that the daylight from above and the artificial light from below are redirected to wash the pier directly below, as well as the lawn adjacent to the pier.

As you walk along the pier and look up through the masts, the sky above is veiled with sparkling light. At night, the stainless steel wire filters the light produced by the spot luminary at the mast's base, creating an inviting environment that has made the pier a popular meeting point for the public to experience the riverfront and its luminous qualities.

**ARCHITECT**
James Carpenter Design Associates

**CLIENT**
City of Chattanooga

**AREA**
n/a

**COST**
n/a

**PHOTOGRAPHER**
Andreas Keller

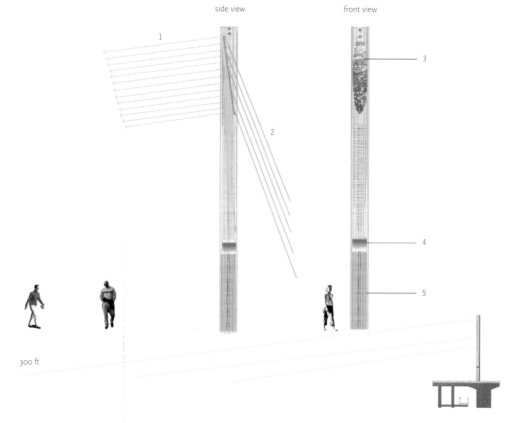

1. Out toward the lawn
2. Softer light down to pier
3. Light reflector
4. BMF – 700. 23-in diameter stainless steel housing narrow spot luminary 1 degree beam angle
5. Stainless steel cylinder

side view

front view

300 ft

Masts' elevations and lighting diagram

# HARLEY-DAVIDSON MUSEUM

Milwaukee, WI, USA   2008

The Harley-Davidson Museum sits on a twenty-acre plot of land near downtown Milwaukee. This site had been previously occupied by a salt manufacturing plant that had contaminated the soil. The design solution involved major earthmoving, including topping the site with four feet of imported soil. The new vegetation was aimed to reintroduce the riparian landscape of the Menomonee River Valley.

The landscape around the building should be understood as part of the museum experience. The design of the museum's surroundings engages the river and the green spaces: a series of river walks planted with native plants connects the man-made landscape with the natural environment. The construction of the museum and its outdoor spaces transform the derelict industrial area into a green space that helps unite the city with the Menomonee Valley. The design of the building and of the landscape reflects the industrial heritage of the site and the image of Harley-Davidson. This is achieved through the extensive use of steel members and rivets, which were conceived as a fundraising mechanism and a way for Harley-Davidson enthusiasts to become part of history.

**LANDSCAPE ARCHITECT**
Oslund and Associates

**LOCATION**
Milwaukee, WI, USA

**CLIENT**
Harley-Davidson Museum

**COLLABORATORS**
Pentagram Architecture (design architect), Hammel, Green & Abrahamson (architect of record), Hammel, Green & Abrahamson and Graef Anhalt Schloemer & Associates (engineers), The Sigma Group and M.A. Mortenson Company

**AREA**
130,000 sq ft

**COST**
USD 75 million

**AWARDS**
2009 Design Honor Award presented by the American Society of Landscape Architects, Minnesota Chapter; 2009 President's Design Award presented by the American Society of Landscape Architects, Illinois Chapter; 2009 Business Journal Real Estate Award presented by *The Business Journal*

**PHOTOGRAPHER**
Oslund and Associates

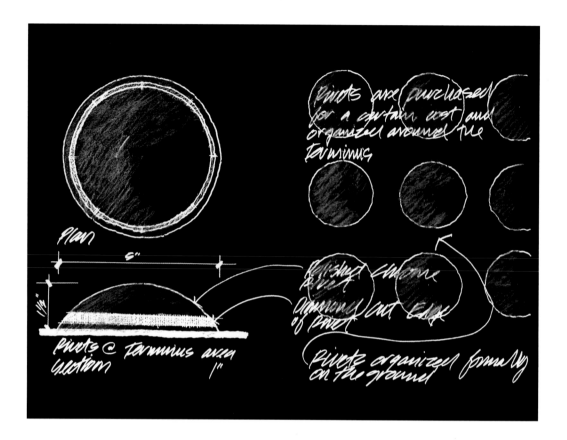

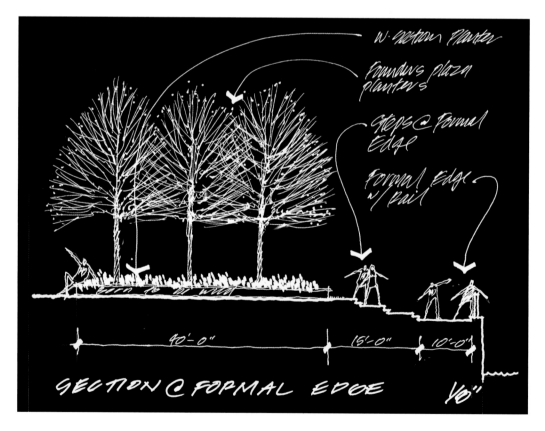

Development sketches

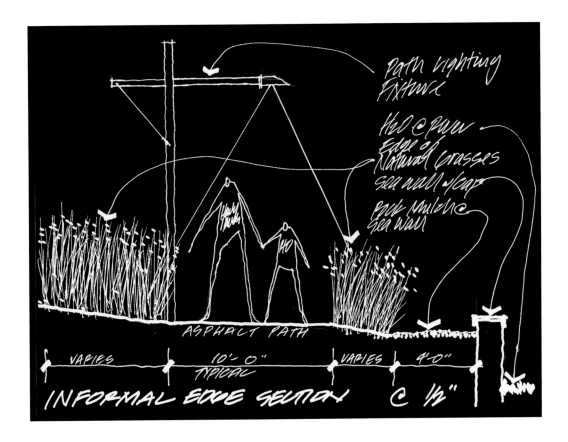

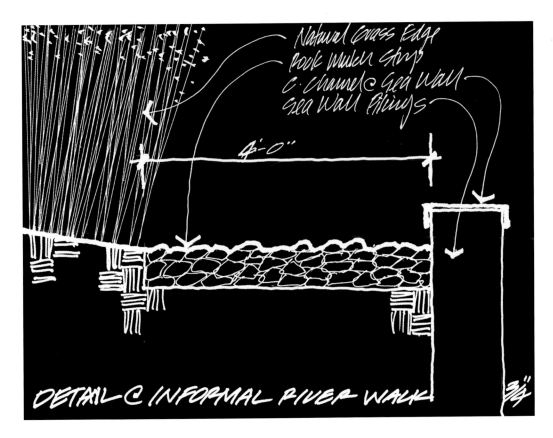

Development sketches

Reclaimed industrial hoppers—now painted Harley-
Davidson orange—act as reference landmarks.
This museum is an achievement of sustainable
reuse, a place for the recollection and creation
of history, as well as a revitalized green space.

# NANSEN PARK

## Oslo, Norway   2008

When the Oslo International Airport moved to its current location in 1998, it left behind a peninsula in need of transformation. The site, about six miles from downtown Oslo, was divided into plots, some of which were sold to developers for housing and office spaces. In 2004, the landscape office of Bjørbekk & Lindheim was commissioned to develop a park that borders the Oslo Fjord on three sides. The goal was to create a functional focus and an identifying landmark for a new community. A strong ecological profile is the foundation of the transformation process: polluted grounds were cleaned, asphalt and concrete were retrieved and reused, and large volumes of earth and rock were used to transform the flat airport area into a landscape with different spatial qualities.

The park has been designed as a dynamic dialogue between the strong linearity of the airport and the soft, more organic forms of the natural landscape that once existed. Seven "arms" enable people to access the park from different sides and integrate areas for recreational activities.

The former terminal building and control tower became the starting point for the water feature that stretches north-south through the park.

**LANDSCAPE ARCHITECT**
Bjørbekk & Lindheim

**LOCATION**
Oslo, Norway

**CLIENT**
Statsbygg and the city of Oslo

**COLLABORATORS**
Atelier Dreiseitl (Water artist/consultant); Norconsult (technical consultant)

**AREA**
49,42 acres (0.25 ha)

**COST**
USD 26,188,980 (NOK 150 million)

**PHOTOGRAPHER**
Bjørbekk & Lindheim

The Festival Plaza and the Strip have been located
to the northwest of the Central Pool, with a clear
reference to the former runway and materials
reflecting its earlier characteristic geology.

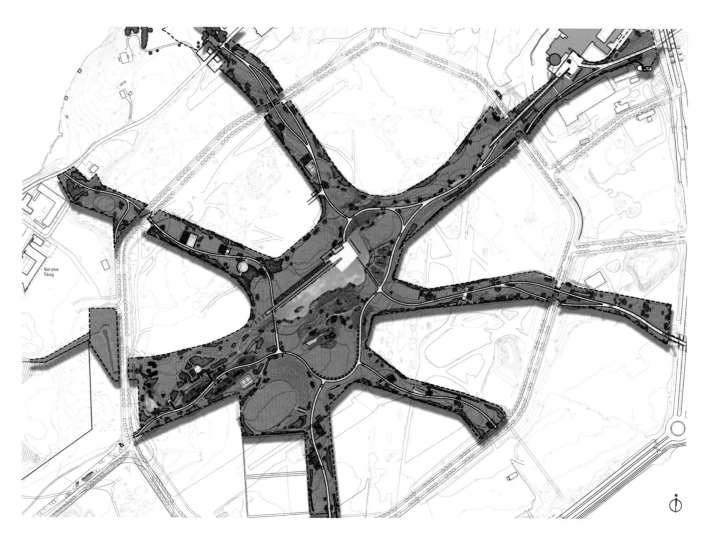

Site plan

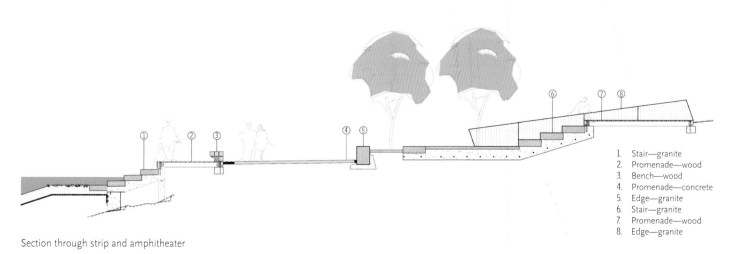

Section through strip and amphitheater

1. Stair—granite
2. Promenade—wood
3. Bench—wood
4. Promenade—concrete
5. Edge—granite
6. Stair—granite
7. Promenade—wood
8. Edge—granite

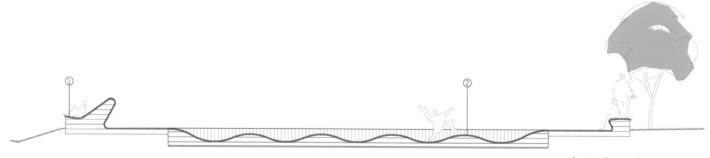

Section through the undulating wood surface

1. Bench—wood
2. Rolling wooden floor

The "arms" consist of volleyball courts, recreation areas made with rubber and wood surfaces for playing, running, and bicycling, large climbing nets, and small reminiscences of the former airport.

narrow water channel runs through rippling
colored glass within a frame of Corten steel
before running down an in-situ concrete water
channel with Corten steel edges and bridges.

# ENVIRONMENTAL RECOVERY
# OF THE PARQUE DE LA RIBERA

Suances, Spain   2006

Located in Suances, in the region of Cantabria, is the Parque de la Ribera. The coastline of this area has been altered over the years, losing its ecological and landscape value. Along the beach, which used to be larger than it is today, was a dune system with a rich vegetation variety that has been progressively disappearing due to the construction of large infrastructures, houses, and other structures.

The project is designed to bring the area to a state as close to what it had originally been as possible. Traffic improvement and the protection of a recovered ecosystem have been the guidelines to bring this project to fruition. The design and construction of a series of paths and boardwalks and a thoughtful selection of plants, have allowed the organization of the various recreational uses and restoration of a dune ecosystem. This was also possible thanks to the complete eradication of invasive plants and the downsizing of a nearby poplar grove.

The result is the recovery and development of an area where a protected ecosystem with high environmental value coexists with the activities of an urban domain.

**DESIGNERS**
Añíbarro Studio of Landscape (David Añíbarro, José Antonio Núñez)

**CLIENT**
Cantabria Environment Department and City of Suances

**COLLABORATORS**
Ángel de Diego, Jesús Varas, Enrique Soto and José Ramón Álvarez.

**AREA**
172,200 sq ft (16,000 m²)

**COST**
USD 526,595 (EUR 386,038)

**PHOTOGRAPHER**
Cantabria government, David Añíbarro

According to the photographic records, in 1953
the main dune system was covering the area that
is currently occupied by the park but had been
neglected through the years. The area, much larger
back then, had significant expanses of vegetation.

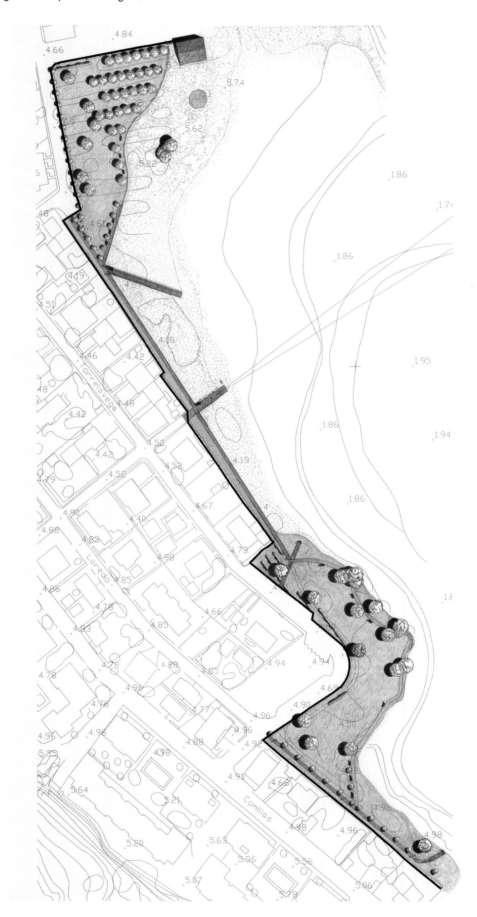

Site plan

Aerial view, 1953

Aerial view, 1988

Aerial view, 2001

Aerial view, Project scheme

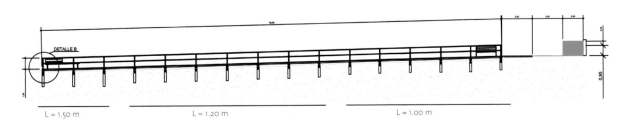

L = 1.50 m          L = 1.20 m                    L = 1.00 m

Section through boardwalk

Different pavements constitute the long walk (875 yards approximately). A curved grassy trail leads to the main concrete path, from which branch out a wooden boardwalk and a sandy path. The latter is configured by arcs that allow getting close to or away from the sea. Where this path ends, a bituminous pavement begins, eventually terminating in a lookout over the San Martin ria.

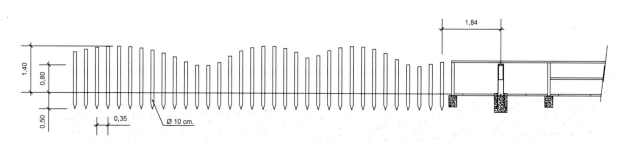

Section through fence to protect the dune system

# PARK OF LUNA

## Heerhugowaard-South, the Netherlands    2008

As part of a larger project called "the City of the Sun," Park of Luna is the result of an attractive recreational development with a naturally purified swimming lake as its central element.

Progressively, a former agrarian landscape south of Heerhugowaard has been transformed into an urban area with housing and natural recreational developments. The "City of the Sun" is a square peninsula located in the center of the plan, a neighborhood with 1,600 homes designed by KuiperCompagnons. It is surrounded by more than 173 acres of water, which can be experienced from the shores of the City of the Sun and also from the embankments of the mainland. During the design and construction process, much attention was devoted to optimizing the water experience, water quality, and accessibility. To this end, various structures were built including a pumping station, a natural purification plant, a dephosphatizing pond, a bridge, and a canoe crossing. Park of Luna is comprised of subareas, each with its own individual character, and is crossed by a system of routes that link the recreational area to the urban region of Heerhugowaard-South.

**DESIGNERS**
HOSPER landscape architects and urban design in collaboration with the municipality, Neelen and Schuurmans and DRFTWD

**CLIENT**
Municipality of Heerhugowaard and HAL-board

**COLLABORATORS**
Water system, planting and nature – Neelen en Schuurmans, IWACO / artists public space – Alon Levin, Jurgen Bey / architects buildings in Park of Luna: Sander Douma Architecten, Schulze en van Dijk, Superflex / architects Subplan 1/2 – Boperai Associates, Jim Lubach architects, Roy Gelders Architects, A+I Architects, INBO, Van den Oever, Zaaijer and Partners, Atelier Dutch, Bear Architects, BBHD Architecten, 19 het atelier architecten and John van Dijk, Architectenburo Hans Wagner, Taneja Hartsuyker architecten and Den Heijer Architecten / architects Subplan 3/4 – v-eld, Venhoeven CS, INBO, Atelier Pro, Arjan Karssen BNO

**AREA**
420 acres (170 ha)

**COST**
n/a

**PHOTOGRAPHER**
Pieter Kers, Aerophoto Schiphol BV / Jan Tuijp (aerial photos)

The Park of Luna has been nominated for the Rosa
Barba European Landscape Prize 2010 and has been
selected, as part of the project "City of the Sun,"
for the European Urban and Regional Planning
Achievement Awards "Special Merit Award," 2010.

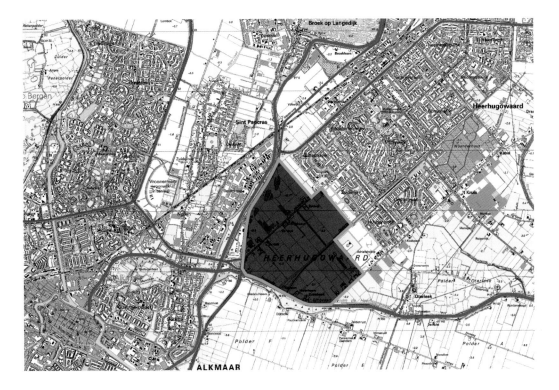

Location map

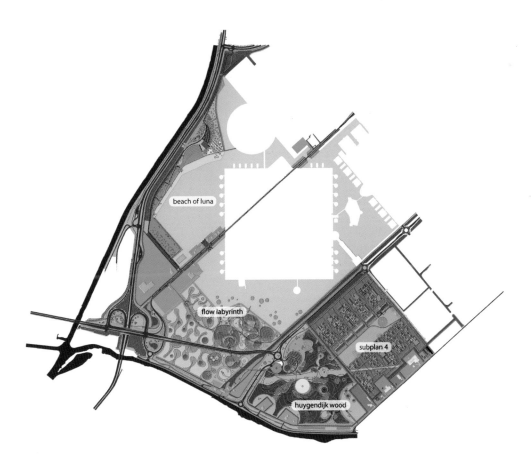

Site plan

The inlet of the water purification plant has been raised above water, level where it is both visible and audible. This infrastructure, part of the large "water purification machine," is a prominent feature in the landscape.

Sketch of the Waerdse Tempel

Sketch of the circulation pumping station

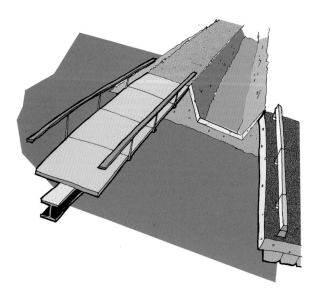

Sketch of the "Middenweg" bridge

# SEAFRONT AND RIVERSIDE DEVELOPMENTS

# RIVA SPLIT WATERFRONT

Split, Croatia    2007

The Split waterfront stretches in front of Diocletian's Palace, the home of a Roman emperor more than 1,700 years ago. Over the centuries, the waterfront has experienced major transformations but has never ceased to be an important feature of the city.

In May 2005, an expert jury awarded the first prize to the work of 3LHD architects at the public competition for the renovation of Split's waterfront. The project follows strict guidelines to preserve the historical and cultural heritage of the site and eliminates all superfluous elements that interfere with the needs of the citizens' contemporary lifestyles. The design consists of a modular grid formed by large concrete blocks with colors that range from white to pale gray. From a bird's-eye view, the arrangement of the blocks creates a pixilated image of a rippling sea.

The row of cafés, restaurants, and pastry shops that for many years had fronted the palace and the buildings along the waterfront was removed from the facades to enable pedestrian movement along the buildings. However, their strong visual identity led to the creation of new outdoor cafés in a more appropriate location. Another very important design element is the natural elements that introduce the unexpected into the project with their flowers, growth, and pleasing scents.

**ARCHITECT**
3LHD

**CLIENT**
The City of Split

**COLLABORATORS**
Numen/For Use - Nikola Radeljkovic, Sven Jonke, Christoph Katzler, Jelenko Herzog, design of urban elements; Ines Hrdalo, landscape design; Novalux - Zlatko Galic and Dijana Galic, light technology design; VOLT-ing - Mladen Zanic, electrical installations; HIDRO-dizajn - Ivo Makjanic, water installations; Boris Goreta, 3D; Zoran Kodrnja, model; Kostruktor Split, contractor; IGH Split, supervision

**AREA**
265,944 sq ft (24,707 m²) (competition entry) / 150,695 sq ft (14,000 m²) (built)

**COST**
USD 15.4 million (EUR 11.3 million)

**PHOTOGRAPHER**
Domagoj Blazevic

The oldest depiction of Split—1,700-years-old Diocletian's Palace with the sea in front

The sea has always been the southern border of the palace

he modular pavement determines the
rangement and the positions of all the
ements of the public space: benches, green
reas, outdoor cafés, sunscreens, and structural
ements such as manholes, water connections,
r distances between light sources.

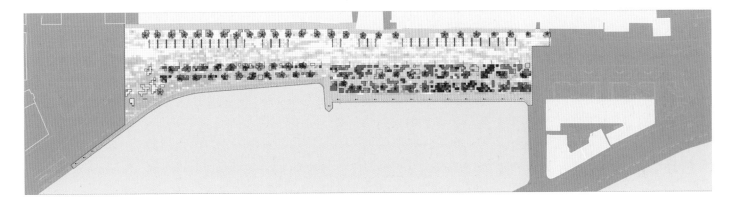

Site plan

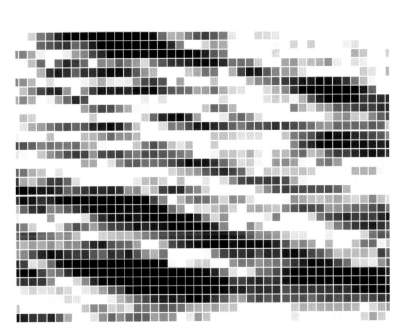

Pixelated sea as a pattern for the new plating

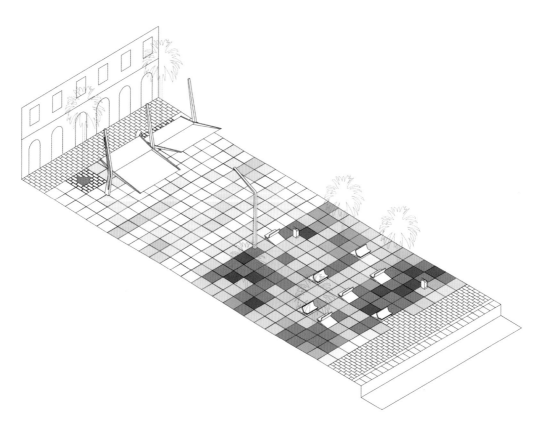

Partial axonometric view of the promenade

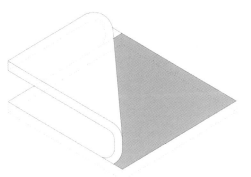
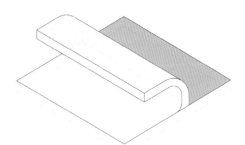
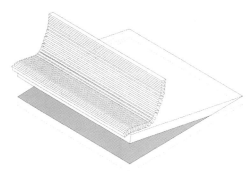

Axonometric views of the benches

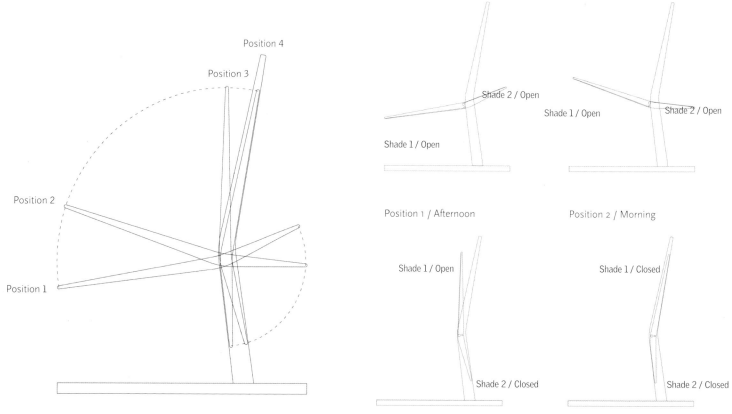

Position 4

Position 3

Position 2

Position 1

Shade 2 / Open

Shade 1 / Open

Shade 1 / Open

Shade 2 / Open

Shade 2 / Open

Position 1 / Afternoon

Position 2 / Morning

Shade 1 / Open

Shade 1 / Closed

Shade 2 / Closed

Shade 2 / Closed

Position 3 / Evening, projections

Position 4 / Winter

Diagram of the sunshade positions

Sunscreens, lights, and other equipment, which used
to have different shapes, sizes, and colors, have
become a part of the image of the city from the sea
and a unique element adapted to the climate, with
the motifs of masts, sailboats, sails, and ships.

503

# TORONTO CENTRAL WATERFRONT

## Toronto, ON, Canada    (ongoing)

The Central Waterfront of Lake Ontario shoreline immediately adjacent to the downtown business district is one of Toronto's most valuable assets. In response to a design competition called Waterfront Toronto, West 8 submitted a comprehensive plan for the Central Waterfront that improves the connection between the city and the lake and produces a continuous, accessible waterfront through a powerful design.

The plan expresses a vision for the Central Waterfront that brings a sustainable, ecologically productive "green foot" to the rich culture of the metropolis. It suggests a new coherence and continuity along the waterfront produced by four seemingly simple gestures that create a new "Multiple Waterfront": the Primary Waterfront—a continuous water edge promenade with a series of pedestrian bridges; the Secondary Waterfront—a recalibrated Queens Quay Boulevard with a new urban promenade and public spaces at the heads of slips; the Floating Waterfront—a series of floating elements that offer new boat moorings and public spaces in relation to the lake; and the Cultures of the City—connections from Toronto's diverse neighborhoods towards the waterfront.

**DESIGNERS**
West 8 and du Toit Allsopp Hillier (DTAH)

**CLIENT**
Waterfront Toronto

**COLLABORATORS**
Schollen & Company, Diamond + Schmitt Architects, Arup, Halsall Associates, David Dennis Design, Mulvey + Banani

**AREA**
2.2 miles length (3.5 km)

**COST**
USD 186 million (Can$ 192 million)

**AWARDS**
2009 Honor Award from the American Association of Landscape Architects (ASLA), 2009 Award of Excellence at the Toronto Urban Design Awards, 2009 Award of Excellence Ontario Builders Awards (2009), 2009 Brit Insurance Design Award Nominee

**PHOTOGRAPHER**
West 8

Master plan

Inspired by the sinuous contours of the shoreline, the geometry of the wave deck is carefully conceived using playful curves that are constantly changing to create ledges for seating and new routes to access the water's edge.

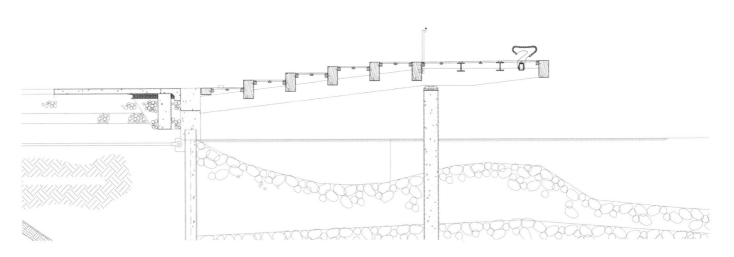

Section through Spadina wave deck

# TJUVHOLMEN

## Oslo, Norway    2010

A new development plan for the waterfront of Oslo has been conceived to turn an old industrial pier into a landscape of islands. Tjuvholmen was annexed to the mainland and incorporated into the dock and harbor area about 100 years ago. With this transformation, Tjuvholmen has regained its original character through the creation of new canals and green public spaces. This transformation project consists of three areas: Odden, the headland, is a dense mixed-use area and an extension of the city center; Holmen is mainly developed as a residential area; and Skjæret is the park and new arts center, carefully integrated into the urban fabric.

The essence of the urban plan for Tjuvholmen is the promenade along the waterfront, which starts at City Hall, northeast of Tjuvholmen, and ends at Olav Selvaag Square. There, three water features reestablish the connection between the city and its waterfront as an integral part of the city's urban culture: a pond made of dark granite, a feature of rippling water in a hollow pillar of *rhomb porphyry* (volcanic stone), and a fountain with six water jets. Water from all three runs in channels through the streets toward the fjord.

**LANDSCAPE ARCHITECT**
Bjørbekk & Lindheim

**LOCATION**
Oslo, Norway

**CLIENT**
Tjuvholmen AS

**COLLABORATORS**
Steen & Lund AS (site gardeners)

**AREA**
64.24 acres (26 ha)

**COST**
n/a

**PHOTOGRAPHER**
Bjørbekk & Lindheim

Along the canal and quaysides, walkways incorporate site-specific designs and provide accessibility for all. There are plenty of benches and a small amphitheater that offers seating right at the edge of the water.

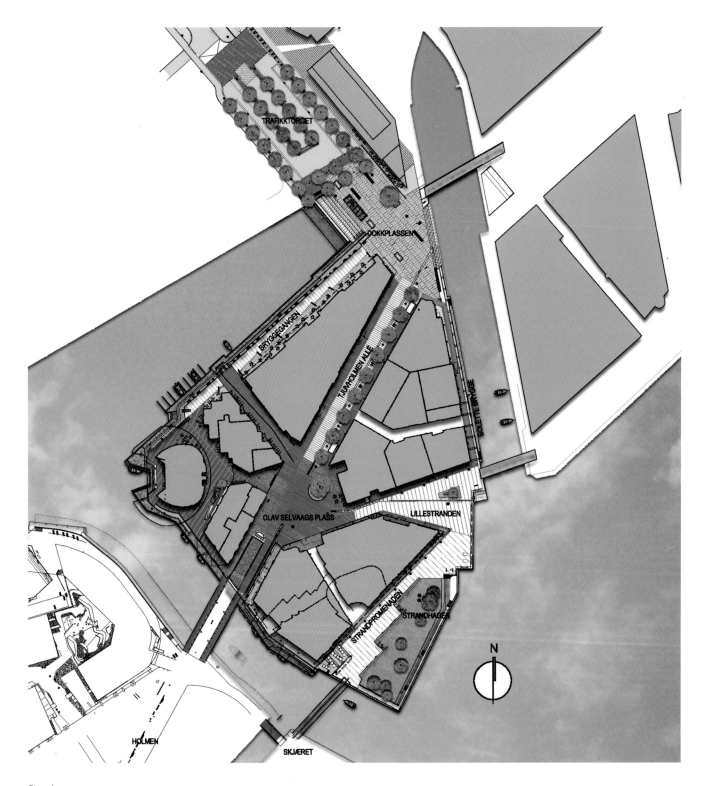

Site plan

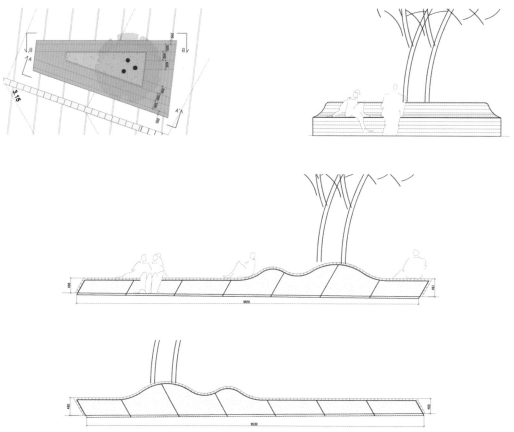

Plan, elevation, and sections of bench and planter

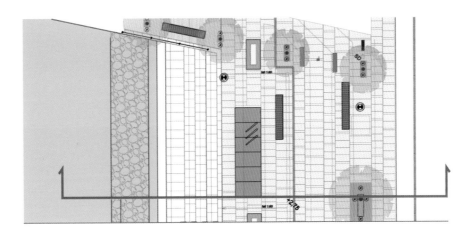

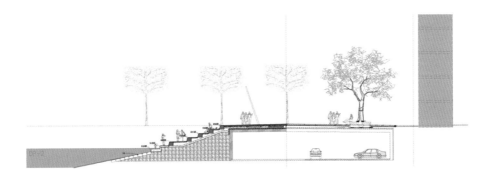

Plan and section of water feature at Dokkplassen

# WEST PALM BEACH WATERFRONT COMMONS

West Palm Beach, FL, USA   2010

Michael Singer Studio with engineers CH2M Hill was selected by the city in 2004 to lead the reimaging process and design for a cohesive West Palm Beach Waterfront Commons. The Singer Studio designed the main park and event spaces, three new floating docks, shaded gardens, two community buildings, a continuous waterfront esplanade, seven specially designed water elements, and an estuarine ecological regeneration area.

The new West Palm Beach Waterfront encompasses over 1/2 mile and 12.5 acres along the Intracoastal Waterway. The design removed and resituated the public library from the base of Clematis Street, opening waterfront views and access to a large public common green space with views to Palm Beach Island. Shaded garden pathways along both North and South Clematis streets have several unique sculptural water gardens. The main central space of the Commons is a large open area to accommodate major downtown events such as the Palm Beach Boat Show and Sunfest. The landing and beach areas result from repositioning Flagler Drive to gain more open space, providing better public access to the water's edge.

**ARTIST AND LEAD DESIGNER**
Michael Singer Studio

**CLIENT**
City of West Palm Beach

**COLLABORATORS**
Carolyn Pendleton Parker at Sanchez & Maddux Inc. and Connie Roy Fisher (landscape architecture), Steve Boruff Architects (architect of record), Barbara Horton and Lee Brandt at HLB Lighting (lighting design), Joan Goldberg (City Project Manager), Ana Aponte, Amy Stelly, and Matt Flis from the West Palm Beach City Planning Department and the Thompson Design Group (planning), Catalfumo Construction, Whiting Turner and Technomarine (Living Docks), Macon Construction (Flagler Drive), Wesco (fountains), CH2M Hill (Design Criteria Phase Project Lead and Initial Site Engineering)

**AREA**
1/2 mile and 12.5 acres

**COST**
USD 30 million

**PHOTOGRAPHER**
Michael Singer Studio, David Stansbury, Catalfumo Construction, Tom Hurst

Completed in 2009, three new docks allow for boat tie-ups and a water taxi to sway visitors into the downtown area. One of the docks includes in-water planters containing native mangroves, spartina, and a visible oyster reef set into the dock surface.

Site plan

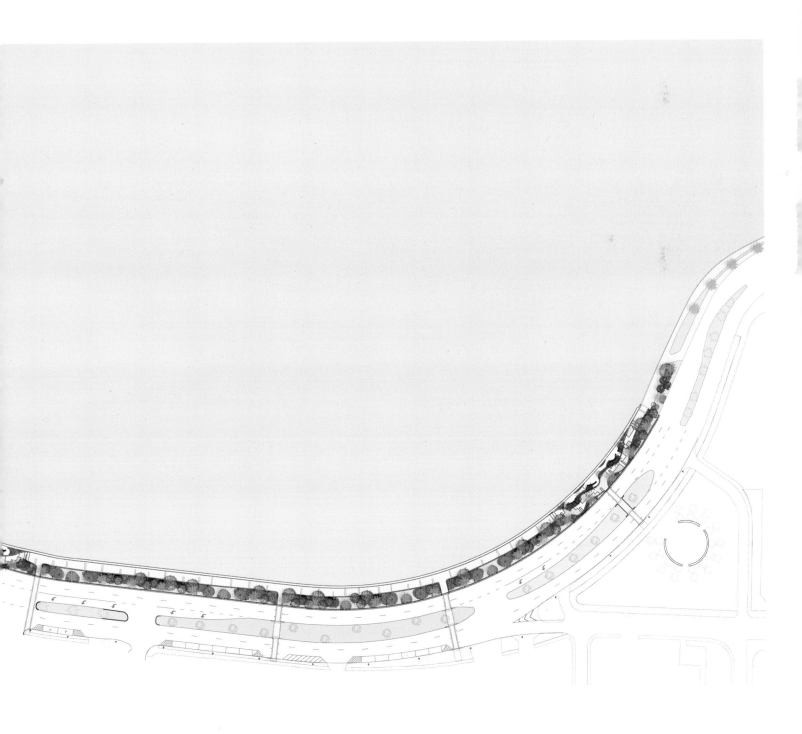

The new esplanade consists of several discreet spaces, including intimate seating areas and small event areas along a continuous bike and pedestrian path, as well as a unique water feature seating bench.

The Lake Pavilion is a glass-walled building that opens onto the Commons with panoramic views of the waterfront. It is utilized as a community center and for special events such as art exhibits, conferences, and weddings.

# MARITIME YOUTH HOUSE

Copenhagen, Denmark   2004

The development of this project faced two challenges. First, the site was polluted, and second, the new facility had to be shared by two very different users: a sail club and a youth house. The sailing club required most of the site to moor their boats, and the youth center wanted outdoor space for the kids to play.

During the first stage of the project, the architectural team realized that the pollution of the soil was caused by heavy metals and therefore stable. This was well received by the designers who saw the opportunity to invest the budget allocated for removing the polluted topsoil—a third of the total budget—into the architecture. It was decided to cover the ground with a wood deck, which solved the issues posed by the conflicting requirements: the deck is elevated high enough to allow for boat storage underneath while providing an undulating surface for the kids to run and play on above. The interior of the building is very low-key—the front room, oriented toward the coastline, is used as a common room where most of the center's daily activities take place.

**DESIGNERS**
BIG + JDS (formerly PLOT)

**CLIENT**
Kvarterløft Copenhagen, Loa Fund
Collaborators: JDS Architects, Birch & Krogboe

**AREA**
21,527 sq ft (2,000 m²)

**COST**
USD 1,975,770 (EUR 1,450,000)

**AWARDS**
2005 Mies van der Rohe Award Special Mention; 2004 Copenhagen Municipality Award for Architecture; 2004 AR+D Award, *Architectural Review*, RIBA London

**PHOTOGRAPHER**
Julien de Smedt, Mads Hilmer, Esben Bruun, Paolo Rosselli

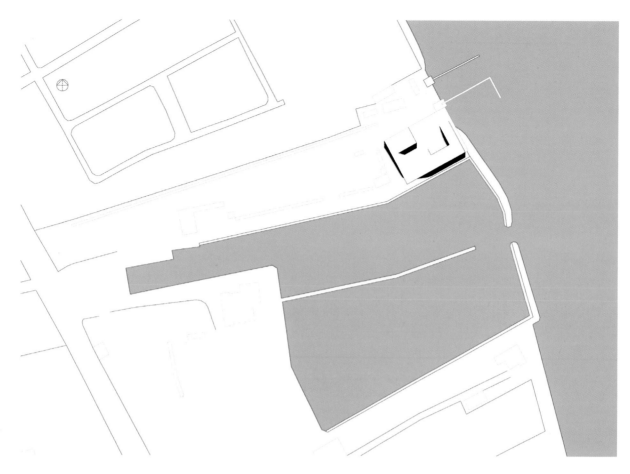

Site plan

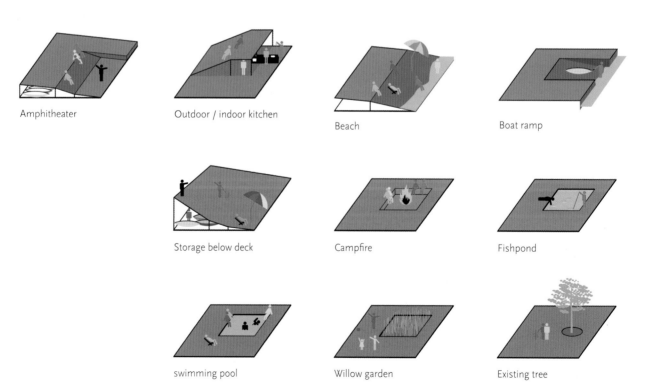

Amphitheater

Outdoor / indoor kitchen

Beach

Boat ramp

Storage below deck

Campfire

Fishpond

swimming pool

Willow garden

Existing tree

Diagrams

The innovative design offers multiple uses to accommodate the different requirements of the Maritime Youth House's occupants. Its flexible program optimizes the interior space as much as the exterior while promoting mobility and social interaction.

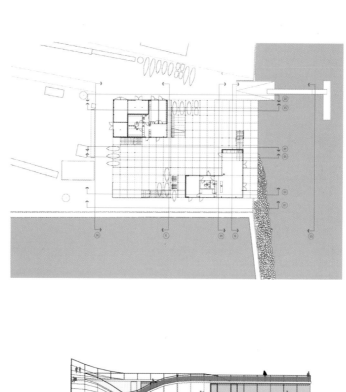

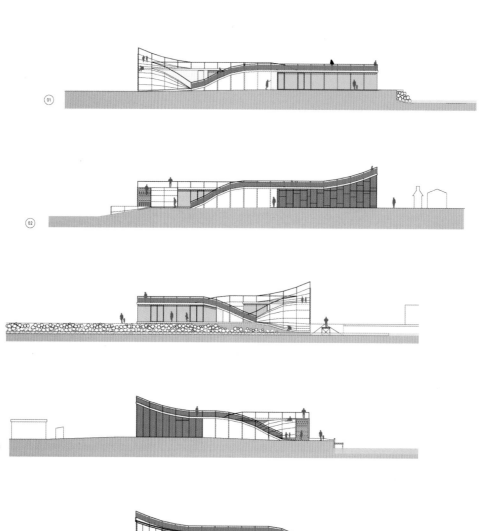

Sections

The use of hard surfaces in the interior contrasts with the wooden exterior, an inversion of what is commonly done (wooden interior with a concrete and asphalt exterior). The Maritime Youth House has therefore gained an additional outdoor "room."

# A SQUARE OUTSIDE THE WALLS

## Santo Stefano al Mare, Italy    2007

The project consisted of converting the entire town center of Santo Stefano al Mare into a pedestrian area and creating public spaces to accommodate social events. The north is delimited by the expansion of the city outside the walls of the historic center, while the south is fronted by the seafront. The program is developed around the old tower and access to the historic center. The organization of the square is based on several elements. Traffic, which dissected the city center, is moved to the periphery. This allows for the creation of a promenade between the city center and the seafront. The design is developed around a thoughtful system of axes that originate at the center of the plaza while enhancing the presence of the old tower. It also avoids any vertical elements that would obstruct the view of the tower from the plaza. The success of the projects lies in the urban reorganization of the city center, which has reinforced the integrity of the historic quarter and established a direct link between the city and the waterfront.

**ARCHITECT**
mag.MA architetture

**CLIENT**
Municipality of Santo Stefano al Mare

**COLLABORATORS**
Edil GA (building contractor)

**AREA**
44,562 sq ft (4,140 m²)

**COST**
USD 956,375 (EUR 701,875)

**PHOTOGRAPHER**
mag.MA architetture

site plan of the historic center—project

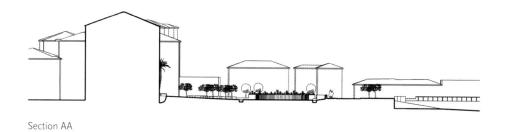

Section AA

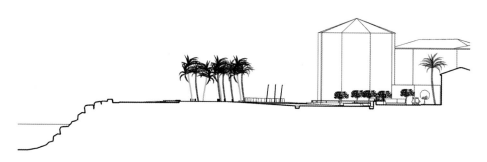

Section BB

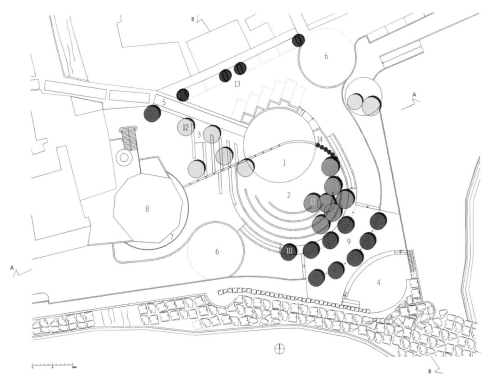

1. Plaza
2. Amphitheater
3. Seating area
4. Vista point
5. Promenade to the historic center
6. Roundabout
7. Moat
8. Old tower
9. Road
10. *Washingtonia*
11. *Cocos nucifera*
12. *Morus platanifolia*
13. *Pittosporum tobira*
14. *Pittosporum variegata*

Enlarged partial site plan

Special attention was paid to the orientation of the new architectural elements in relation to existing landmarks, the visual connections between the plaza and the tower and those between the plaza and the waterfront, as well as accessibility and materials.

# MANGFALLPARK ROSENHEIM

Rosenheim, Bavaria, Germany    2010

In the city of Roseheim, the relocation of an industrial area has allowed for the extension of the urban development to the banks of the rivers Inn and Mangfall. Mangfallpark is part of this development and was built to accommodate the state garden show in 2010. Mangfallpark's central feature is a boardwalk system and eight bridges that reinforce the unique character of the landscape in the area and bring nature closer to the city. The Mühlbach creek which had been built over was uncovered to become a green corridor between the city and the Inn River. The new construction included in the development plan will allow for urban gardens along the creek. The northern-most part of the promenade boardwalk ends in an twenty-six-feet-long platform, which offers a remarkable view from the rivers all the way to the Chiemgau Alps. Also, a nicely shaped bridge, the Nickl-wiesen boardwalk, crosses the Hammer-bach, which has been transformed into a kayak course. The gravel islands in the stream affect the river flow while at the same time creating areas for the visitors to sit. These recreational contributions are complemented by playgrounds and sports fields.

**LANDSCAPE ARCHITECT**
A24 Landschaft

**LOCATION**
Rosenheim, Bavaria, Germany

**CLIENT**
Landesgartenschau Rosenheim

**COLLABORATORS**
Joachim Naundorf, Carole Blessner, Holger Fahlenbrach, Steffan Laub, Ulli Heckmann, Stephan Huber

**AREA**
140,000 sq ft (13,000 m²)

**COST**
USD 12,763,502 (EUR 10 million)

**PHOTOGRAPHER**
Hanns Joosten

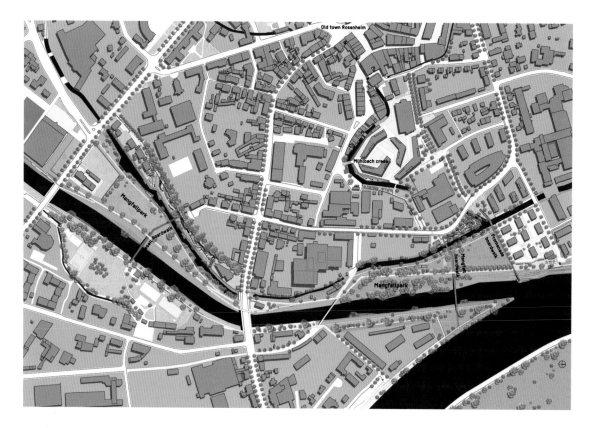

Site plan

Elevations

The boardwalk forms the backbone of the new park and is a multifunctional architecture hybrid—it's a ramp, bridge, promenade, viewing point, and seat, all in one.

# MADRID RIO

Madrid, Spain   2011

Madrid RIO is an urban improvement project along the banks of the Manzanares River in Madrid, initiated by moving underground a stretch of the ring highway adjacent to the city center. The design proposal of West 8 urban design & landscape architecture & Mrio Arquitectos was the only submission to the invited international competition to resolve the urban situation exclusively by means of landscape architecture.

The design is founded on an idea they termed "3 + 30," a concept that proposes dividing the 197.68 acres urban development into a trilogy of initial strategic projects that establish a basic structure for any future projects. Initiated in part by the municipality as well as by private investors and residents, a total of forty-seven subprojects have been developed, the most important of which include the Salón de Pinos, Avenida de Portugal, Huerta de la Partida, Jardines de Puente de Segovia, Jardines de Puente de Toledo, Jardines de la Virgen del Puerto, and the Parque de la Arganzuela. In addition to the various squares, boulevards, and parks, a series of bridges was built to improve connections between the urban districts along the river.

**DESIGNERS**
West 8 urban design & landscape architecture, Mrio Arquitectos Asociados

**CLIENT**
Madrid City Government

**COLLABORATORS**
Ginés Garrido Colomero (project management)

**AREA**
198 acres (80 ha)

**COST**
USD 381.95 million (EUR 280 million)

**AWARDS**
*Condé Nast Traveller* Innovation and Design Awards (nominee 2009)

**PHOTOGRAPHER**
Municipality of Madrid, Jeroen Musch

One of the dominating motifs for the Madrid
Rio project is water, and developments along the
Manzanares River are based on the different emotions
and landscapes in context with this element.

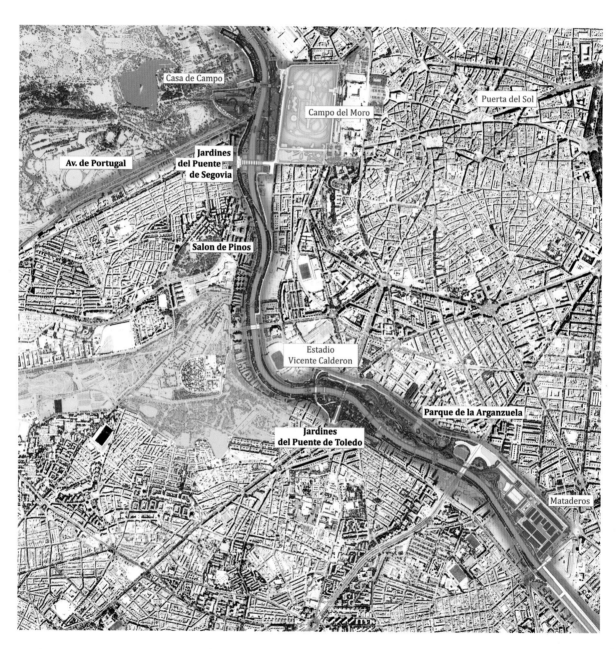

Site plan

In contrast to the usual technical pedestrian infrastructure, the "Shell" bridges create a place where the river can be really experienced. Designed as a massive concrete dome with a rough texture, the ceilings feature mosaics created by Spanish artist Daniel Canogar.

The selection of trees, shrubs, and ground cover provides the embankments of the Manzanares River with a natural and sculptural character and allows for a clear structuring of the different spaces with a variety of uses.

# PROJECTS

# ARANZADI PARK

Pamplona, Spain  2008 (in progress)

The site, located between Pamplona's city center and two adjacent neighborhoods, features a landscape of lush vegetation. The project is intended to recuperate the energy of a meander through nature, in terms of its environmental effects on the flora and fauna, and to reestablish the link between man and nature. It promotes the balance between public spaces and the restoration of native flora and planting of organic crops along the riverbed of the Arga River. A comprehensive analysis of the site's topography and of the flooding pattern suggested that the park and the river should work together to create a seasonal landscape. The project uses the existing elements of the site and enhances its history and its process of transformation through its seasonal changes, in which water plays an important role. Flooding clearly defines the character of the Aranzadi Park, especially along the river, where the design incorporates solutions such as filtering and slowing hedges, meshes covered with vegetation that serve the same purpose, and walls that force surface flows. This constant transformation of the meander presents the opportunity to change the relationship of people with the river.

**LANDSCAPE ARCHITECT**
aldayjover arquitectura y paisaje

**LOCATION**
Pamplona, Spain

**CLIENT**
Pamplona Municipality

**COLLABORATORS**
David Garcia, Consultores BIS Arquitectos (structures), Maurici Ginés, Artec3 (lighting), Ernesto Calvo, PyP (systems), Jochen Scheerer, ASEPMA (purification), David Maruny, ABM (hydráulics), Fernando Benedicto, Benedicto Gestión de Proyectos (budget)

**AREA**
215,278 sq ft (20,000 m²)

**COST**
USD 8,799,184 (EUR 6,457,642)

**PHOTOGRAPHER**
aldayjover

Aerial view of Aranzadi Park

Streets and paths diagram plan

| | | | |
|---|---|---|---|
| ▬▬ | Main street | 1. | "Vuelta de Aranzadi" |
| | | 2. | "Travesera de Aranzadi" |
| ▬▬ | Secondary street | 3. | Arga trail |
| | | 4. | Woods trail |
| — | Side streets | 5. | Recreational garden trail |
| | | 6. | Wildlife garden trail |

Project plan diagram

| | | |
|---|---|---|
| ▭ | No intervention area | 75,376 m² |
| ▬ | Low intervention area | 77,077 m² |
| ▬▬▬ | Standard level intervention area | 67,159 m² |
| | A. No maintenance area | 65,952 m² |
| | B. Low maintenance area | 77,077 m² |
| | C. Standard level intervention area | 76,583 m² |

General plan

| | |
|---|---|
| ▬ | Natural bed of the Arga River in Aranzadi |
| ▨ | Woodland in flood area |

Zoning diagram

| | | |
|---|---|---|
| ▨ | 1a. | Municipal school orchard |
| ▨ | 1b. | Municipal school facilities |
| ▨ | 2. | Experimental orchard |
| ▨ | 3. | Production orchard |
| ▨ | 4. | Community garden |

Vegetation diagram

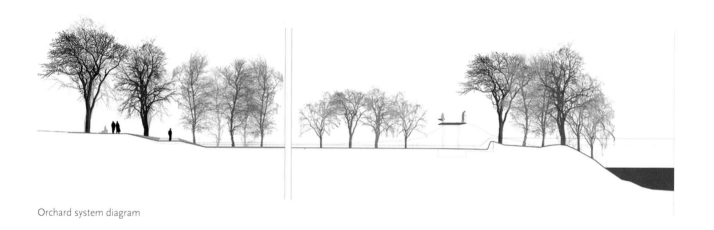

Orchard system diagram

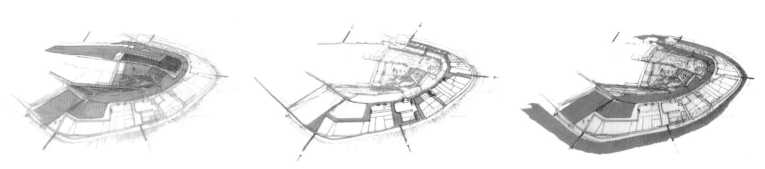

Water system diagram                    Vegetation diagram                    Orchard  system diagram

# DRAVA RIVER 2012

## Maribor, Slovenia    2010

An international architecture competition was called for the redevelopment of Maribor's urban fabric as the key setting of the European Capital of Culture in 2012. EstudioOCA proposes a riverfront redevelopment aimed to improve urban life and spatial appropriation. There are no grand gestures, but, rather, the design has been developed within the existing context and does not seek to make unnecessary alterations. One of the key goals was to make the site legible and thus permit multiple uses of the spaces. Long, wide walkways function as a continuation of the city, leading to the adjacent accessible river banks, always vibrant, with people enjoying the spaces.

The selection of materials is simple, consisting of the existing granite paving, new, low-maintenance pavements of stone or concrete, and wood (ideally from a local source). The planned spaces are mostly continuous and accessible to people with disabilities. The project includes a simple pluvial water filtration system in the form of the planted areas, all of which have been designed to allow for effective and economic purification. The Judgment tower pool is connected to the triangular pool of the ancient fort, which is an ornamental receptacle in the event of storms.

**LANDSCAPE ARCHITECT**
estudioOCA

**CLIENT**
Municipality of Maribor

**COLLABORATORS**
Julia Coquelle, Pietro Giannini, Emanuela Miceli, Carlos Principe, Jimi McKay, Nicola Marmugi

**AREA**
56.8 acres (23 ha)

**COST**
n/a

**RENDERINGS**
estudioOCA

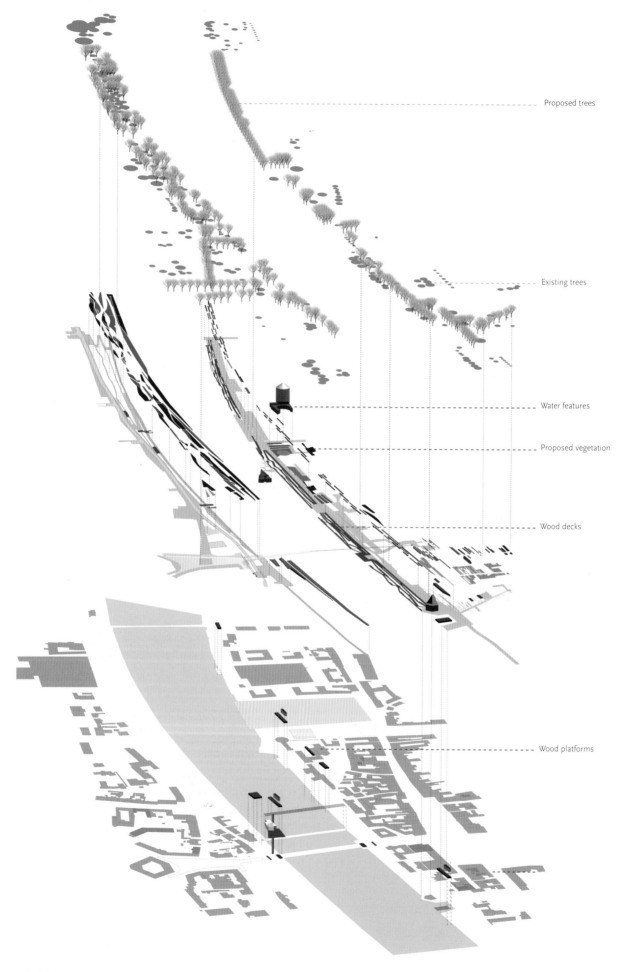

Proposed trees

Existing trees

Water features

Proposed vegetation

Wood decks

Wood platforms

Exploded axonometric view of design layers

The project emphasizes the existing potential of the site. With minimal alterations, the Drava embankments offer an array of activities that range from taking the ferry under the main bridge to relaxing on a wood deck and enjoying the spectacle of the river.

Site plan

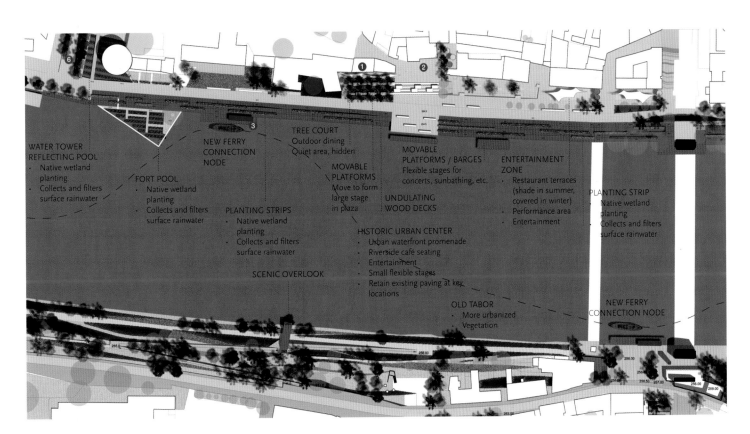

WATER TOWER
REFLECTING POOL
· Native wetland
  planting
· Collects and filters
  surface rainwater

FORT POOL
· Native wetland
  planting
· Collects and filters
  surface rainwater

PLANTING STRIPS
· Native wetland
  planting
· Collects and filters
  surface rainwater

NEW FERRY
CONNECTION
NODE

SCENIC OVERLOOK

TREE COURT
Outdoor dining
Quiet area, hidden

MOVABLE
PLATFORMS
Move to form
large stage
in plaza

UNDULATING
WOOD DECKS

HISTORIC URBAN CENTER
· Urban waterfront promenade
· Riverside café seating
· Entertainment
· Small flexible stages
· Retain existing paving at key
  locations

OLD TABOR
· More urbanized
  Vegetation

MOVABLE
PLATFORMS / BARGES
Flexible stages for
concerts, sunbathing, etc.

ENTERTAINMENT
ZONE
· Restaurant terraces
  (shade in summer,
  covered in winter)
· Performance area
· Entertainment

PLANTING STRIP
· Native wetland
  planting
· Collects and filters
  surface rainwater

NEW FERRY
CONNECTION NODE

Detailed site plan

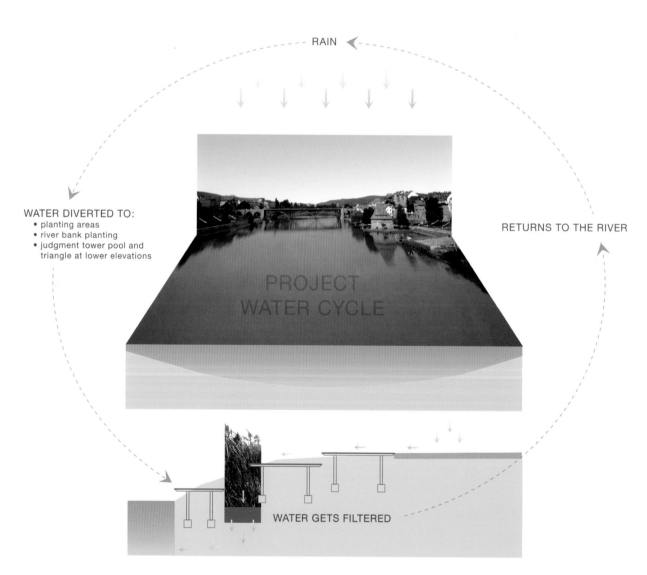

RAIN

WATER DIVERTED TO:
• planting areas
• river bank planting
• judgment tower pool and
  triangle at lower elevations

RETURNS TO THE RIVER

PROJECT
WATER CYCLE

WATER GETS FILTERED

Water cycle diagram

# GARDEN OF FORGIVENESS

Beirut, Lebanon   2003

The Garden of Forgiveness is located at the heart of Beirut's Central District and is surrounded by historic churches and mosques. A prewar puzzle of a landscape held within the borders of Lebanon, at one moment complete and at the next moment shattered, the Garden is representative of the context's fragility. To provide easy access to the Garden from the city, it was clear that parts of the dug-out site had to be covered again. This led to the design of a series of ramps and terraces that keep clear of the most important archaeological features. Throughout the garden, the archaeological remains of five successive civilizations are both revealed and reinterpreted in a new context. Symbolical elements of the Lebanese landscape impart a timeless feel, while the contemporary interpretation of landscape focuses on the creation of communal symbols. Overall, the design of the Garden is conceived in the tradition of the paradise garden, which incorporates water, pathways, and a strong geometric layout. It is meant to be an oasis in the midst of the urban hubbub, a place for both solitary reflection and communal gathering.

**LANDSCAPE ARCHITECT**
Gustafson Porter

**CLIENT**
Solidere

**AREA**
2,47 acres (1 ha)

**COST**
n/a

**RENDERINGS**
Gustafson Porter, Richard Davies (scale model)

Master plan

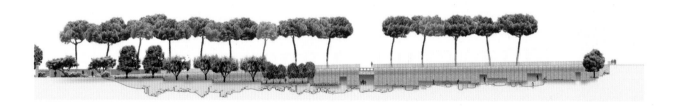

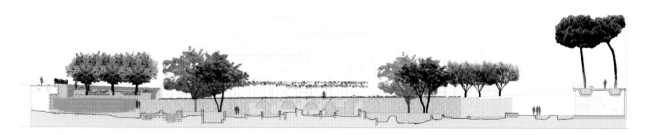

Sections

# KAOHSIUNG PORT STATION
# URBAN DESIGN COMPETITION

Kaohsiung, Taiwan    20011

The competition, promoted by the City Government of Kaohsiung, is intended to transform the derelict site occupied by old rail yards and a port station into a connecting point of the urban fabric. The site currently separates two important areas of the city. The client demanded that the program include new developments to accommodate the expansion of the city, while highlighting the cultural heritage of the site. For this reason, the majority of the buildings had to be retained as historical monuments.

The winning proposal includes the construction of mixed-use urban blocks with commercial areas, and the conversion of industrial buildings into artist studios and galleries. Rail yards, rail lines, and station buildings are integrated in a new linear park, the central feature of which is an indoor-outdoor museum about the industrial history of the area and the city. The design of the park draws from the rail lines and prioritizes a continuous pedestrian and cyclist route along the length of the park. One key element of the design is the land bridge: a combination of bridge and landmark structure that accommodates museums and other facilities.

**ARCHITECT**
De Architekten Cie

**LOCATION**
Kaohsiung, Taiwan

**CLIENT**
City Government of Kaohsiung

**COLLABORATORS**
Rosetta Elkin of RSE Landscape,
Branimir Medic and Malone Chang +
Yu-lin Chen Architects

**AREA**
38 acres (15.42 ha)

**COST**
n/a

**RENDERINGS**
De Architekten Cie

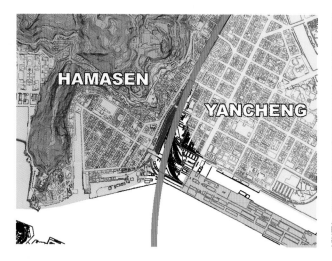

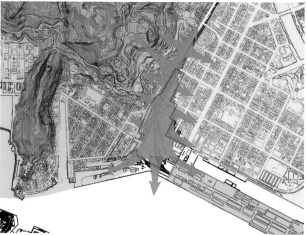

Barrier

The green heart connects districts

Conceptual diagrams

Multi-use housing blocks

Adaptive reuse of existing
industrial buildings

Landscape / cultural
heritage

Zoning diagram

The design strategy sensibly extends the existing urban structure to the site with an appropriate programmatic mix of commercial and residential uses based on the specific location of each block.

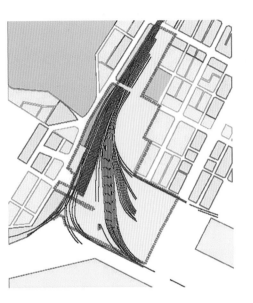

Competition site

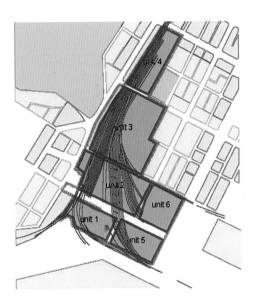

Commercial units

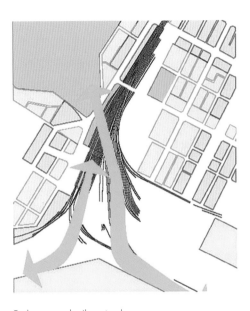

Park zone and railway tracks

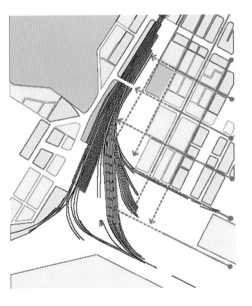

Extension of the grid

Programmatic diagrams

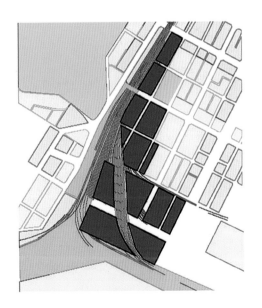

Building plots

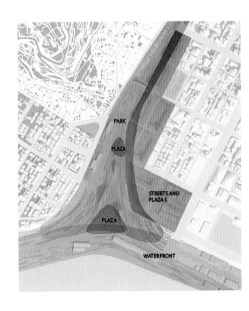

Zoning concept

Objectives:

By strengthening the connection between the Hamasen and Yancheng district, we can transform two disparate parts of the city into a unified area that has at its heart a large urban park.

A north-south connection enables users to travel seamlessly between the waterfront and the southern Gushan district to the north and provides a link between the waterfront and Shou Mountain.

To control vehicular traffic across the site by restricting it to the Wufu, Gongyuan, and Linhai roads.

To promote pedestrian and cyclist accessibility across the site through park and landscape paths and connections. Although vehicular access from secondary roads ends at the park edge, the pedestrian walkways continue to cross the site.

Analysis and strategy

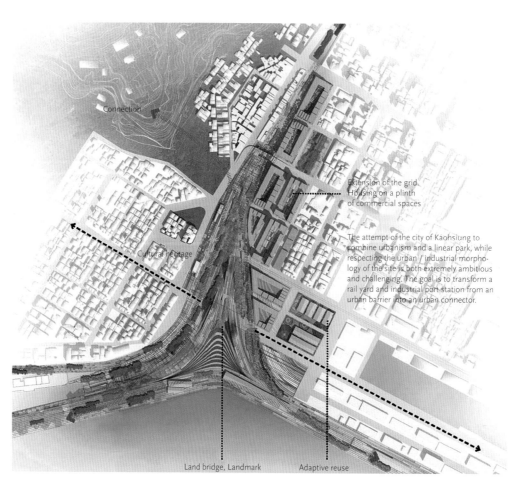

Goals

"As the economy of Taiwan gradually transforms from its manufacturing and industrial past to one based on cultural production and tourism, our proposal can make a significant contribution to the evolution of the city of Kaohsiung." *Jason Lee and Patrick Koschuch*

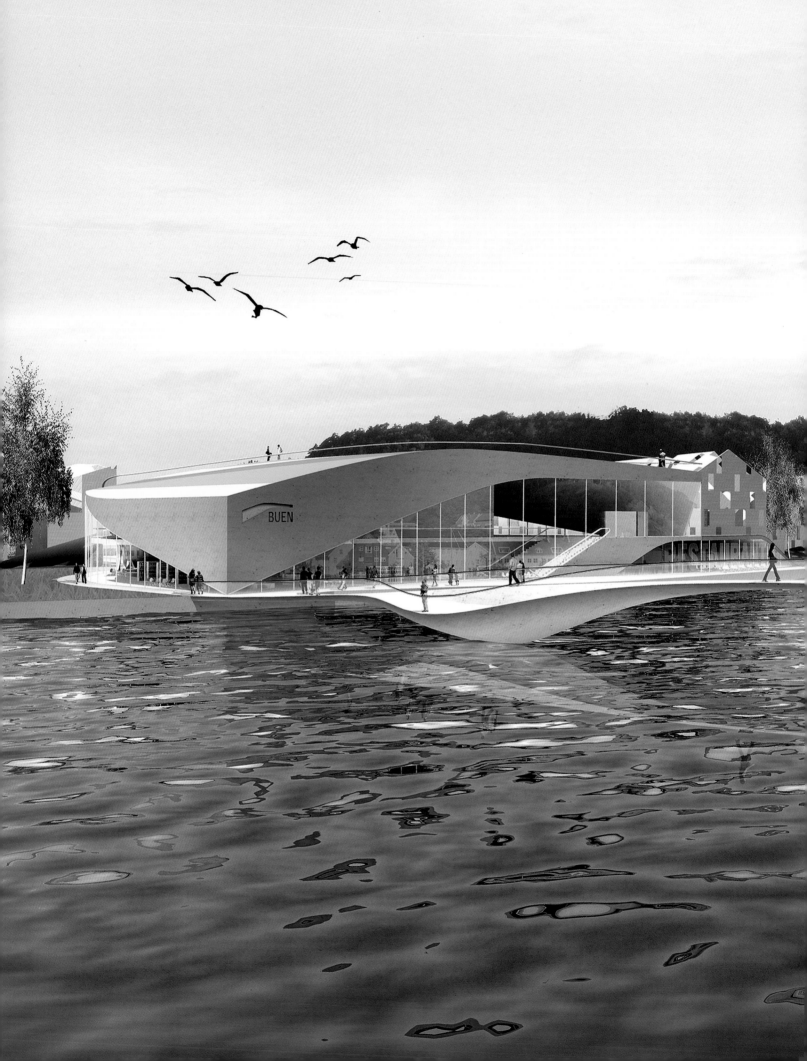

# BUEN

## Mandal, Norway

Buen ("arch" in Norwegian) is a green mantle that, as if blown by a breeze, rises from the ground to make room for a cultural center.

3XN conceived the master plan for the expansion of the town of Mandal to the opposite side of the river. It includes, in addition to a cultural center integrated with a hotel, various constructions for residential and commercial use. These constructions, which take as a reference the scale and proportions of the traditional Norwegian wood house, reflect the character of the existing town, while their layout, organized around the cultural center, takes advantage of the view of the river and the town. The project is also designed to minimize motorized traffic and to promote narrow pedestrian and bicycle pathways, as well as green zones.

In contrast with the small scale and coherent planning of the housing and commercial buildings, the cultural center is an architectural landmark that opens to the river embankment. Its undulating roof provides additional green space for the residents and hotel guests.

**ARCHITECT**
3XN

**CLIENT**
Halse Eiendom

**AREA**
322,917 sq ft (30,000 m²)

**COST**
USD 46,680 (255 illion DRK)

**AWARDS**
1st Prize in invited competition (2007)

**RENDERINGS**
3XN A/S

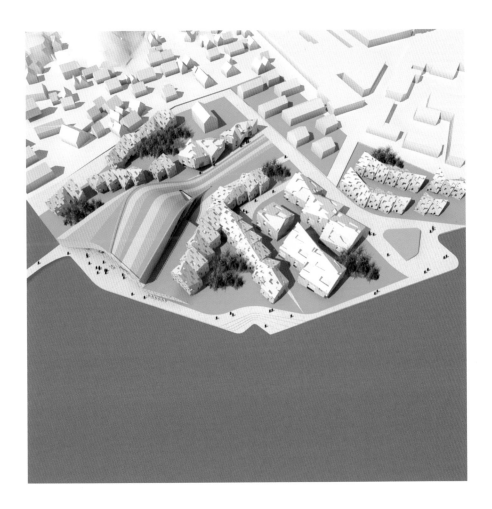

Site plan

Winners of an invited competition to redevelop the industrial waterfront of the town of Mandal, 3XN proposes to turn the brown field into a new cultural complex linked with the town center via a new bridge—also designed by the architectural team.

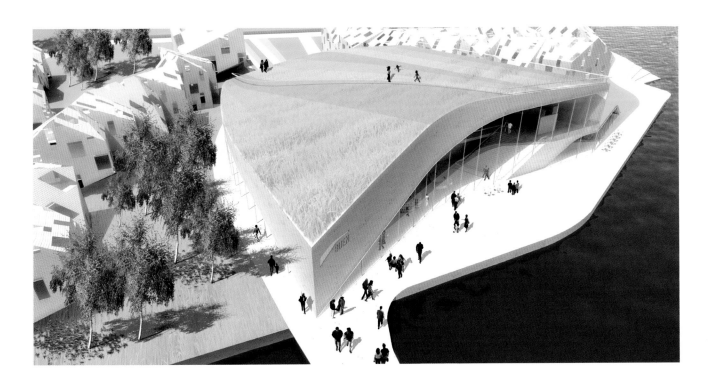

# GOVERNORS ISLAND

## New York, NY, USA   (ongoing)

West 8's winning design competition entry for Governors Island's future open space envisions a park filled with natural elements: a landscape that is local, regional, and national in stature—the "Un-Central park." The park will provide places to relax, play sports, and explore amid the historic monuments shaped by the 400-year history of Governors Island, framed by extraordinary views of the Statue of Liberty and the skyline of the city.

The hills will be programmed within a variety of aquatic experiences, as well as interactive and educational exhibits. Concepts for the southern part of the island consist of wet marshes for ecological, recreational, and pedagogical uses, and a unique habitat for wetland flora and fauna. Free wooden bicycles will be made available to explore the various tracks, allowing the visitor to discover the site from a kinetic perspective.

At the northern section—a National Monuments district—existing historic buildings will be repurposed and used for educational, cultural, and recreational uses. The Summer Park and the terraces in front of Liggett Hall will offer a variety of seasonal botanical park experiences and leisure facilities.

**LANDSCAPE ARCHITECT**
West 8 urban design & landscape architecture

**LOCATION**
New York, NY, USA

**CLIENT**
GIPEC (Governors Island Preservation and Education Commission)

**COLLABORATORS**
Rogers Marvel Architects, Diller, Scofidio + Renfro, SMWM, Urban Design

**AREA**
90 acres

**COST**
n/a

**AWARDS**
2011 Award of Merit, New York Chapter of the American Society of Landscape Architects (ASLA)

**RENDERINGS**
West 8

# Directory

**3LHD**
Zagreb, Croatia
www.studio3lhd.hr

**3XN**
Copenhagen, Denmark
www.3xn.dk

**A24 Landschaft**
Berlin, Germany
www.a24-landschaft.de

**Affleck + de la Riva architectes**
Montreal, QC, Canada
www.affleck-delariva.ca

**aldayjover arquitectura y paisaje**
Barcelona, Spain
www.aldayjover.com

**ANNABAU Architecture
and Landscape**
Berlin, Germany
www.annabau.com

**Añíbarro Studio of Landscape**
Santander, Spain
www.anibarropaisajismo.com

**Arkitekt Kristine Jensens Tegnestue**
Aarhus, Denmark
www.kristinejensen.dk

**ASPECT Studios**
Adelaide, SA, Australia
Melbourne, VIC, Australia
Sydney, NSW, Australia
Shanghai, China
www.aspect.net.au

**Atelier Dreiseitl**
Überlingen, Germany
Beijing, China
Portland, OR, USA
www.dreiseitl.net

**Basurama (designer)**
Madrid, Spain
www.basurama.org

**BIG + JDS (formerly PLOT) (designer)**
Copenhagen, Denmark
New York, NY, USA
www.big.dk / www.jdsa.eu

**Bjørbekk & Lindheim**
Oslo, Norway
www.blark.no

**Choi Ropiha, Perkins Eastman,
PKSB Architects (designers)**
Manly, NSW, Australia
www.chrofi.com

**Cornelia Oberlander Architects**
Vancouver, BC, Canada
www.corneliaoberlander.ca

**De Architekten Cie**
Amsterdam, the Netherlands
www.cie.nl

**Deltavormgroep**
Utrecht, the Netherlands
www.deltavormgroep.nl

**Dirtworks Landscape Architecture**
New York, NY, USA
www.dirtworks.us

**Dominique Perrault Architecture**
Paris, France
www.perraultarchitecte.com

**DRFTWD**
Amsterdam, the Nethlerlands
www.drftwd.nl

**du Toit Allsopp Hillier (DTAH)**
Toronto, ON, Canada
www.dtah.com

**Ecosistema Urbano**
Madrid, Spain
www.ecosistemaurbano.com

**estudioOCA**
Barcelona, Spain
San Francisco, CA, USA
Bangkok, Thailand
www.estudiooca.com

**Gustafson Porter**
Seattle, WA, USA
www.gustafson-porter.com

**HIK Ontwerpers**
Utrecht, the Netherlands
www.hik-ontwerpers.nl

**HM White Site Architects**
New York, NY, USA
www.hmwhitesa.com

**HOSPER landscape architects**
Haarlem, the Netherlands
www.hosper.nl

**idealice**
Vienna, Austria
www.idealice.at

**James Carpenter Design Associates**
New York, NY, USA
www.jcdainc.com

**Karres en Brands**
landschapsarchitecten
Hilversum, the Netherlands
www.karresenbrands.nl

**made associati_ architettura**
e paesaggio
Treviso, Italy
www.madeassociati.it

**mag.MA architetture**
Arma di Taggia, Italy
www.mag-ma.it

**McGregor Coxall**
Manly, NSW, Australia
www.mcgregorcoxall.com

**Mia Lehrer + Associates**
Los Angeles, CA, USA
www.mlagreen.com

**Michael Singer Studio**
Delray Beach, FL, USA
www.michaelsinger.com

**Mikyoung Kim Design**
Boston, MA, USA
www.mikyoungkim.com

**Nabito Architects**
Barcelona, Spain
www.nabit.it

**Neelen and Schuurmans**
Utrecht, the Netherlands
www.nelen-schuurmans.nl

**OBRA Architects**
New York, NY, USA
www.obraarchitects.com

**Office of James Burnett**
Solana Beach, CA, USA
Houston, TX, USA
www.ojb.com

**Oglo**
Paris, France
www.oglo.fr

**Oslund and Associates**
Minneapolis, MN, USA
www.oaala.com

**PLANT Architect**
Toronto, ON, Canada
www.branchplant.com

**Rehwaldt Landschaftsarchitekten**
Dresden, Germany
www.rehwaldt.de

**Roberto Ercilla Arquitectura**
Vitoria-Gasteiz, España
www.robertoercilla.com

**Robin Winogrond
Landscape Architect**
Zürich, Switzerland
www.winogrond.com

**Rogers Marvel Architects**
New York, NY, USA
www.rogersmarvel.com

**SLA**
Valby, Dermark
www.sla.dk

**Taylor Cullity Lethlean**
Carlton, VIC, Australia
Adelaide, SA, Australia
www.tcl.net.au

**Tom Leader Studio**
Berkeley, CA, USA
www.tomleader.com

**Tonkin Liu**
London, UK
www.tonkinliu.co.uk

**Topotek 1**
Berlin, Germany
www.topotek1.de

**TROP: terrains + open space**
Bangkok, Thailand
www.tropstudio.com

**Turenscape**
Beijing, China
www.turenscape.com

**West 8 urban design &
landscape architecture**
Rotterdam, the Netherlands
www.west8.nl